T0386693

THE HATS OF THE QUEEN

Thomas Pernette
Illustrations by Jason Raish
Foreword by Alastair Bruce of Crionaich OBE

Hardie Grant

B O O K S

FOREWORD

By Alastair Bruce of Crionaich OBE

Hats catch the eye and, in this book, Thomas Pernette catches our eyes and focuses them on the woman who has provided more work for milliners than any other.

In ancient times, rulers were adorned with apparel that enhanced their elevated status. Pharaohs, chiefs and monarchs were generally garlanded around their temples with jewelled bands of gold, treating the leader's head as a sort of deified temple, especially following the Christian act of anointing.

Queen Elizabeth II was anointed and crowned on 2 June 1953, with the crown made for Charles II in 1661 by the royal goldsmith Robert Vyner. In that moment she was made somehow different and invested with symbols from a millennium of tradition.

But she was also the child of a generation and class that never left the house without being properly hatted. Throughout her 96 years, 70 of them as sovereign, almost every public engagement she attended was honoured with a new hat.

Hats can say a great deal. They are perfect for a high-profile woman who is slight of stature, especially when the strategy behind her wardrobe is to be seen. Indeed, the Queen always provided a clear intent to her dressers: 'We need to be seen to be believed.'

Once the hat was placed upon the Queen's head, in Her Majesty's dressing room, she set off on a day of engagements in a high-roofed state car. Through lunch and tea, the hat remained fixed, until she was home again and sat before the dressing-room mirror once more.

So, practicality was always vital in a lifetime of being smart in Britain's changeable weather, to say nothing of the extremes of temperature she encountered during her tours as Head of the Commonwealth.

In common with her mother before her, Queen Elizabeth used her hats as a communication tool. After the abdication in 1936, Queen Elizabeth The Queen Mother made pastel shades and floppy-brimmed hats her leitmotif, to strengthen a kingdom through war. So, too, with elegance, confidence and splendid effect, the Queen moved from childlike sparkle to mature glint, always crowned with the powerful symbol of a hat.

CONTENTS

INTRODUCTION   6

THE MODERN LITTLE GIRL   22
London, 1933

THE CALL TO ARMS   26
Windsor, February 1945

A LESSON IN STYLE   30
Cape Town, April 1947

A PRINCESS IN PARIS   34
Paris, 15 May 1948

TROOPING THE COLOUR   38
London, 7 June 1951

MORE HATS FOR MISS DONALD   42
Canberra, 17 February 1954

THE NEW YORK MARATHON   46
New York, 21 October 1957

MARGARET GETS MARRIED   52
London, 6 May 1960

THE CHARM AFTER THE STORM   56
Karachi, 1 February 1961

FLOWER POWER   62
Epsom, 31 May 1961

THE SPAGHETTI HAT   66
Berlin, 27 May 1965

UNCLE DICKIE   70
Isle of Wight, 26 July 1965

CROWNING CHARLES   74
Caernarfon, 1 July 1969

ONE STEP CLOSER TO THE PUBLIC   78
Sydney, 1 May 1970

THE DUKE OF WINDSOR QUIETLY PASSES AWAY   82
Paris, 18 May 1972

HIGHCLERE   86
Chantilly, 16 June 1974

THE CHRYSANTHEMUM THRONE   90
Kyoto, 10 May 1975

TWO HATS FOR THE PRICE OF ONE   96
London, 7 June 1977

THE LADIES OF THE BAHAMAS   100
Nassau, 19 October 1977

A HIGH-RISK MISSION   104
Lusaka, 27 July 1979

A NIGHTMARE IN THE SUNSHINE   108
Marrakech, 27 October 1980

THE WEDDING OF THE CENTURY   112
London, 29 July 1981

WHO TRIED TO KILL THE QUEEN?   116
Wellington, 14 October 1981

THE QUEEN ON THE OTHER SIDE OF THE WORLD   120
Tuvalu, 27 October 1982

CHARMING COMPANY 124
Amman, 27 March 1984

MADE FOR CHINA 128
Badaling, 14 October 1986

THE TALKING HAT 132
Washington, 14 May 1991

ANNUS HORRIBILIS 138
London, 24 November 1992

THE MAGNUM OPUS 142
Channel Tunnel, 6 May 1994

THE WORLD MOURNS DIANA 148
London, 5 September 1997

END OF AN ERA 152
Portsmouth, 11 December 1997

HAZARDS OF THE JOB 156
Kuala Lumpur, 21 September 1998

GREETINGS FROM NORWAY 160
Oslo, 30 May 2001

THE FUTURE IS IN SAFE HANDS 164
London, 12 June 2006

GARDEN PARTY 168
London, 11 July 2006

THE DUCHESS OF CORNWALL 172
Braemar, 2 September 2006

HATS OFF TO CARLA 176
Windsor, 26 March 2008

BACK TO THE EMIRATES 180
Abu Dhabi, 24 November 2010

ALL BETS ARE OFF! 184
London, 29 April 2011

A RETURN TO PEACE 190
Dublin, 17 May 2011

DEAREST OBAMAS 194
London, 24 May 2011

AN INVINCIBLE ARMADA 198
London, 3 June 2012

THE LILAC REVOLUTION 202
The Vatican, 3 April 2014

LA VIE EN ROSE 206
Paris, 7 June 2014

AN ANTI-BREXIT HAT? 210
London, 17 June 2017

FIRST SOLO OUTING WITH MEGHAN 214
Chester, 14 June 2018

THE ORDER OF THE GARTER 218
Windsor, 17 June 2019

THE NATION'S HERO 222
Windsor, 17 July 2020

WE'VE MISSED YOU 226
Salisbury, 15 October 2020

FAREWELL, PHILIP 230
Windsor, 17 April 2021

APPENDICES 234

INTRODUCTION

Until the 1940s, all women – or at least nearly all – wore hats. It was extremely rare for a woman to leave the house without one: at the time, going out bareheaded was seen as a mark of extreme poverty, or at least of inexcusable negligence. The richest women would change their hats depending on the time of day, or according to their mood. Hats were a staple of women's wardrobes, as journalist and fashion historian Jacqueline Demornex recounts: 'Cocktail dresses were always accompanied by an elegant hat, and there was no such thing as a party that wasn't filled with sumptuous flowers and feathers. The ideal setting for a new hat? Shopping, of course, but restaurants worked well too. Once seated, a pretty woman could no longer show off her dress, but her hat remained on display throughout the meal. This magical object had the power to exalt her face

Page 3 Elizabeth II at Windsor in May 1979.
Opposite This beret with ostrich-feather pompom was designed by Norman Hartnell, November 1947. The execution was entrusted to Aage Thaarup.

and make-up, and to theatricalise her slightest gesture: be it lifting her veil, smoking, drinking or smiling. Each movement became wreathed in mystery. It was enough to make one sigh: "Oh hat, what would women be without you?"[1]

A FAMILY HISTORY

The British royal family is not known for starting fashions. Having ascended the throne in 1910, King George V, Elizabeth II's grandfather, was a conservative at heart who hated music, dancing and even women wearing nail varnish. Flanked by such a husband, Queen Mary had little chance to be a trendsetter. 'She was far more interested in fashion than most people imagine, however, and I think she sometimes secretly aspired to casting aside the hats and dresses with which she had become associated,' Mabell Ogilvy, Countess of Airlie, her maid of honour, suggests in her memoirs.[2] Such an aspiration would have been in vain, however. In the early 1950s, when Queen Mary was over 80, she was still wearing her classic plumed hats. In London, a former milliner,

Miss Gallaway, almost as old as Queen Mary herself, was the only one who still knew how to make them.[3]

Known for her cheerful, natural disposition, her daughter-in-law Elizabeth Bowes-Lyon, Duchess of York, followed fashion trends but was careful not to start them. When the milliner Aage Thaarup met her for the first time in the early 1930s, she was the mother of two adorable little girls: Elizabeth and Margaret. 'I remember her smile, and her incredible warmth. She gave off an impression of great sensitivity and benevolence that set one immediately at ease.'[4] After becoming Queen, and then Queen Mother, Elizabeth Bowes-Lyon remained determined to do credit to her country through her clothing and hats throughout her life. 'Fittings with the Queen Mother were always very enjoyable affairs,' recalls another royal milliner, Claude Saint-Cyr. 'She would receive us in the morning, and we were always greeted by a plentiful buffet, which included salmon, toast, and *café au lait* on account of our being French. She spoke the language very well, as she would demonstrate by reciting "Le Loup et l'Agneau" (The Wolf and the Lamb), or other fables by La Fontaine.'[5]

Of all the women in the royal family, it was Princess Margaret who best mastered the art of hat-wearing. She was the first to employ the milliner Simone Mirman, whose services Elizabeth II then quickly

called upon too. Margaret was a demanding customer with a touch of the whimsical about her: she once entrusted Mirman with creating a hat modelled on a Moroccan carpet she loved. Her milliners' efforts were always well rewarded, however, since in the 1950s and 1960s being associated with the Queen's younger sister was a sure-fire way to achieve widespread publicity. When Mirman launched her collections every year, the press – incredulous – would print her most extravagant models[6] alongside the question: 'Will Princess Margaret really wear such a hat?'[7]

Elizabeth II, for her part, was never a fashion victim. 'She was too intelligent to concern herself with haute couture. She was certainly no fashionista. She loved anything that was timeless,' explained one of her dressmakers.[8] Setting aside her personal tastes, the Queen knew she must steer clear of anything that might be seen as too commercial, new or audacious. For was she not the very incarnation of an age-old institution? And were her hats not – to use the historian Robert Lacey's expression – 'substitutes for the crown'?

THE NITTY-GRITTY OF THE ROYAL HAT

The Queen was doubtless the woman who wore the most hats during her lifetime. She had an excellent eye for them, too; she knew what she wanted and what suited her.

Her hats had a very strict remit: they must ensure that she could be

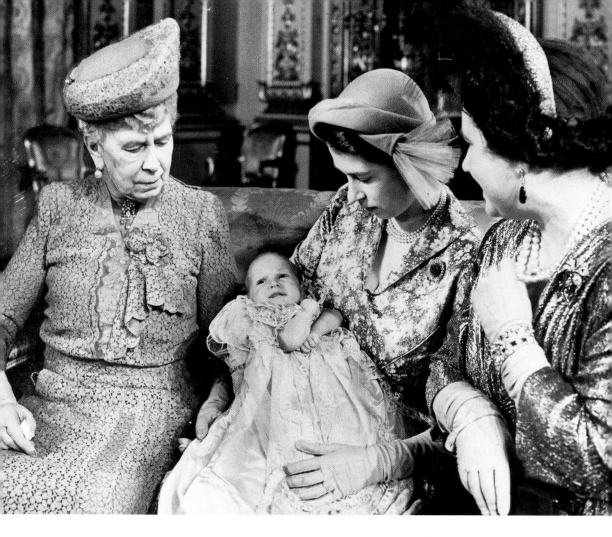

Queen Mary, Elizabeth II holding Princess Anne – during her christening – and the Queen Mother, on 21 October 1950 at Buckingham Palace.

seen from a distance, by as many people as possible. As such, they were very often brightly coloured, as were her clothes. They needed to be neither too high nor too wide, so that they did not get in the way when she was entering or leaving a vehicle. And lastly, they must not hide her face.

Elizabeth II wore a hat for every official outdoor engagement, even in the gardens of her own royal residences, such as for her garden parties. After 18 hours, if she was attending a state dinner or banquet the Queen would usually swap her hat for a tiara. In private and while on holiday, she would either go bareheaded or wear a headscarf, particularly if she was out riding.

'The Queen may well be one of the richest women in the world, but she is also one of the thriftiest. Take her hats, for example,' a journalist wrote with amusement in 1982.[9] Elizabeth II was indeed a professional recycler. Angela Kelly, her senior dresser since 1996, explained that the life expectancy of her outfits could

Elizabeth II wears a fur hat
in Charlottetown, Canada, in October 1964.

extend as far as 25 years: 'After two or three outings, the public and the media will already be familiar with a particular item, so we either look for ways to alter it, or it becomes something she wears in private at Balmoral or Sandringham.'[10]

Her hats had several lives, too. Some would make their mark only after their second or third appearance; a beret with pink bellflowers, for example, caused a sensation during the Silver Jubilee in 1977, even though it had actually made its first appearance the year before, during the opening ceremony of the Olympic Games in Montreal. A blue hat adorned with yellow daisies, accused of being anti-Brexit in 2017, became so famous that it was impossible for the Queen to wear it a second time as it was. The solution: to transform it by replacing the daisies with a large blue bow. Wearing a hat several times was almost a duty.

What do the hundreds, or even thousands, of hats made for the Queen since she was a young child tell us? They are testament to a particular season or era. Pillbox hats were succeeded by berets; turbans gave way to Breton hats. The materials of which they were made also provide precious insights into the history of taste and attitudes. Having been omnipresent at the beginning of the Queen's reign, felt

and velvet grew increasingly rare. Traditional straws were replaced with a vegetable fibre: sisal or parasisal. While these materials did confer a certain lightness upon the hats, they also attested to a widespread impoverishment of the sector. Faced with dwindling demand – who wears a hat every day any more? – entire industries collapsed and some straws even disappeared. The emerging ecological awareness also had an effect. The use of certain feathers is now forbidden, such as feathers from birds of paradise, and in 2019 the Palace announced that it would no longer use furs.

In terms of their style, however, the Queen's hats became increasingly understated. For several years, the Queen wore the same style of hat, with just a few rare exceptions: a hybrid model somewhere between a boater and a cloche hat. Stella McLaren, personal milliner to the Queen, was charged with decorating them with flowers and feathers. During her last years, in her nineties, these lavish headpieces conferred a certain jauntiness, almost an eternal youth, upon the Queen.

IN HER MAJESTY'S SERVICE

At the beginning of her reign, two dressmakers shared the distinct honour of dressing the Queen: Norman Hartnell, who gained worldwide fame by designing her coronation gown in 1953, and Hardy Amies. In 1970 they were joined by

Above, from top Five of the Queen's milliners: Philip Somerville, Marie O'Regan, Aage Thaarup, Sadie Box and Frederick Fox.

Opposite A hat being made in Philip Somerville's studios, and worn by the Queen in London in 1996.

a third designer, Ian Thomas, a former student of Hartnell. To make Her Majesty's indispensable hats, all three called upon the services of the leading milliners of the time.

Unlike hatters, who produce hats on an assembly line, milliners design one-off pieces. They are therefore just as much artisans as they are artists. The profession has long been dominated by women; in the interwar period, a number of female milliners shot to celebrity-like stardom. In London, producing hats for the royal family represented the pinnacle of a career. Unfortunately, because of the lack of archives, the work of many of these milliners has fallen into oblivion. Who, for example, will remember Kate Day, Rose Vernier, Sadie Box or, more recently, Valerie Lee, who was employed by Ian Thomas in the 1970s and 1980s? A handful of these creators, more fortunate or perhaps more adept at seizing the limelight, who were not satisfied with merely receiving the precious royal warrant (a mandate that established them as an official supplier to the Crown), have succeeded in leaving their mark on fashion history. One might cite Aage Thaarup, a milliner of Danish origin who settled in London in 1932 and made hats for Princess Elizabeth from 1947 onwards. Having earned an excellent reputation at the beginning of the Queen's reign, Thaarup profited from the incredible buzz generated by her first Commonwealth trips in the 1950s.

At the same time, two women made their debuts as royal milliners: Claude Saint-Cyr and Simone Mirman. The former embodied Parisian chic. With one foot in France and the other in the United Kingdom, Saint-Cyr presented her first collection in

London in 1953: 'I was travelling backwards and forwards between Paris and London a lot. I loved that city. At the time, you could already see a difference between French women – who were beginning to go out without hats, even in formal settings – and their British counterparts, who would wear a different hat depending on whether they were going for lunch, five o'clock tea, or cocktails, as in France back in the 1930s and 1940s.'[11] Saint-Cyr was also held in high esteem at Buckingham Palace for her hairstyling talent, in addition to her hats.

Simone Mirman, originally from Lorraine, began working for the royal family in 1952 while her husband, Serge Mirman, was organising Christian Dior's first London shows. The couple rented a house on Chesham Place, next to Belgrave Square, and used the ground floor as a workshop and salon where they could receive clients. 'The first time she felt like a true milliner was when she managed to make a hat that brought out the best in her mother's somewhat tricky face,' recalls her daughter Sophie Mirman, with amusement. 'She would even sometimes refuse to sell a client a hat if she thought it didn't suit them.'[12] A close friend of Norman Hartnell, Simone Mirman became the queen of turbans, which made a great comeback in the 1970s.

Frederick Fox, for his part, was Australian. During a career spanning 35 years, he made almost 350 hats for the Queen. Having trained in Sydney, he moved in the late 1950s to London, where he landed a job at Otto Lucas, a highly sought-after studio. It was there that he met Philip Somerville, who became famous in the 1980s for his 'Flying Saucer' hats. Yet it was Hardy Amies who opened the doors to Buckingham Palace for Fox, in 1968. 'I am so tired of seeing my beautiful clothes ruined by terrible hats,' Amies barked at Fox, in an attempt to convince the Australian to work with him.[13]

Of all the Queen's milliners, Marie O'Regan is probably the one who had the most atypical career. Born in Armenia in 1925, she lost her father when she was just a baby. She and her mother emigrated to France and settled in Paris, where they lived very modestly. Despite her talent for drawing, Marie decided against attending art school because of the expense. Instead, she turned her attention to hats. After her apprenticeship, she worked in Gilbert Orcel's studio for a while before setting off for England to learn English: 'I didn't for a

Opposite, clockwise from top left The Queen at Ascot in 2016; in Mexico in 1975; in Berkshire in 1992; and on the Isle of Man in 1989. Philip Somerville's 'Flying Saucer' hat (bottom left) is emblematic of the 1980s, as the turban had been in the 1970s.

Elizabeth II attends a show during London Fashion Week for the first time, on 20 February 2018. On her left sit Anna Wintour and the Queen's senior dresser, Angela Kelly.

second imagine I would end up staying, not to mention one day be making hats for the Queen.'[14] She ended up making more than 200, however, primarily for Thomas. She became close friends with him, as his letters to her demonstrate: 'I greatly appreciate and admire your incredible artistic vision. You have breathed new life into me!'[15]

THE TRICKS OF THE TRADE

'Hats are always chosen to add the finishing touch to an outfit. They provide an interesting demonstration of the work that goes on between the milliner, the Queen and the dressmaker, and of the relationship between the three of them,' explains Caroline de Guitaut.[16]

Milliners work according to sketches that the dressmaker produces for the Palace. Sometimes they receive very precise instructions about the hat, while at other times they are given completely free rein. In turn, the milliner proposes,

In turn, the milliner proposes, suggests, designs (many milliners prefer to shape the material directly) and creates the first models; these form the basis for a selection of prototypes that are presented to the Queen. Fox summed up the process: 'I would go to the Palace with my three or four choices, present them and explain that it was important to only consider the form. I would then suggest that we make one of them in the same fabric as the dress or dye one of the others, making my own preference very clear.'[17]

The Queen's fittings always took place in the presence of her senior dresser, who was in charge of her wardrobe. This key position was long occupied by the indispensable Margaret MacDonald – known by the affectionate nickname Bobo – who had been at Elizabeth II's side since childhood. Fox, who got on perfectly well with MacDonald despite being a little wary of her, called her 'the dragon' in secret. Aided by her assistant Peggy Hoath, Miss MacDonald paid attention to the tiniest details. She passed away at Buckingham Palace in 1993, at the age of 89. Peggy Hoath was then promoted to senior dresser, and the Palace recruited a new assistant: Angela Kelly. A force to be reckoned with, Kelly, who was also invited to the fittings, did not hold back in asserting her opinion, especially when she judged the models presented to be unflattering. Having grown used to decades of affected silence, the dressmakers and milliners were dumbfounded. 'I was their worst nightmare,' admits Kelly, who took over from Hoath when she retired.[18]

The first fitting – and hence generally the first meeting with Elizabeth II – was an intimidating moment for any milliner, serving as a kind of test. For her first fitting, Simone Mirman arrived, armed with her boxes of hats, at the front gates of Buckingham Palace. Although they did let her in, the staff kindly explained that she should arrive at the rear entrance the next time. Terrified at the thought of committing a faux pas, Fox did not stop talking. Having been duly briefed, they both dreaded the moment when they would need to take their leave, since under no circumstances could one turn one's back on the Queen. Mirman almost stepped on a corgi. When it came to Fox, however, Elizabeth II put him out of his misery. Seeing how petrified he was, the sovereign turned towards Miss MacDonald and exclaimed, 'Oh, Bobo, would you kindly pass me the shoes that go with this?', giving the poor milliner the chance to take his leave.[19]

Yet these moments were also an opportunity to meet the Queen up close in a private setting. 'She is the nicest client I've ever met; and I've seen many women be very difficult when they come to order hats,' explained O'Regan.[20] 'She's someone I could have been friends

accent during fittings.'[21] The bond with Philip Somerville was even closer. Indeed, whenever they were unable to meet in person, the Queen and her milliner would write to each other: 'Thank you for your letter, in which you describe how well your business is doing. I was very pleased to learn that you will still be able to work for me. I know how difficult business can be these days, especially when you need to order specific fabrics for me, not to mention that I must be the only person that always wears a hat.'[22]

In the mid-2000s Angela Kelly undertook a radical shake-up of operations at the royal household. As well as Her Majesty's personal dresser, Kelly was appointed adviser and curator in charge of jewellery and insignia, as well as style adviser to the Queen. Having never studied fashion or worked in a fashion house, she became the first 'household' designer. In this role, she designed the Queen's outfits as well as her hats, supported by the milliner Stella McLaren, who made them. Faced with the enormity of the task, however, she also frequently called upon the designer Stewart Parvin to make suits and coats, and Rachel Trevor-Morgan was entrusted with making hats from 2006 onwards.[23]

FOLLOW THE HATS

As well as shedding light on the history of fashion, Elizabeth II's headpieces offer an interesting lens through which to look back at visits, trips, jubilees, meetings and much more. Some pieces hit the newspaper headlines, while others were the subject of heated debate or even mockery. Other, more understated pieces show us what was going on behind the scenes at Buckingham Palace, behind the official décor and duties, which can never fail to fascinate. If only they could speak …

Faced with such an abundance of choice, selecting which headpieces to consider was no easy task. Nor, at times, was identifying their designers. For some of the hats presented in this book, the author has yet to uncover all their secrets. So be it. As hundreds of hats lie in the wardrobes of Buckingham Palace, the accounts of their finest hours speak volumes. Selected for their originality, these little works of art take us on a journey through time.

Previous spread Elizabeth II holds her hat on the deck of *Britannia* during an official visit to Canada in June 1959.
Opposite The Queen in Southampton, 2004.

THE MODEL LITTLE GIRL

The princesses were growing up fast. The elder, Elizabeth, would soon celebrate her seventh birthday; her younger sister, Margaret Rose, was about to turn three. It was time for the little girls to have a governess. Their mother, the Duchess of York, believed she had found a rare gem in her native Scotland. The candidate, Marion Crawford, who had just turned 23, was appointed on a trial basis for a month. A few days before Easter, carrying a small bag in her hand, she presented herself nervously at Royal Lodge, the York family's residence in Windsor.

Some may find it surprising that, within the royal family, such responsibility was conferred upon someone unknown, who was very young and had little experience. Of course, Elizabeth was never expected to become queen; her uncle the Prince of Wales was in robust health, and no one doubted that he would one day get married. The little girls were nonetheless third and fourth in line to the throne, respectively. King George V and Queen Mary were concerned by the choice of governess, which they deemed risky. Breaking with custom, the sovereigns invited themselves round for tea with the York family shortly after the governess's arrival. 'No one had said anything, but I got the sense they had come to observe me,' Miss Crawford later

THE PRINCESSES COULD NOT HAVE BEEN DRESSED MORE SIMPLY.

Marion Crawford

explained. 'I was sure that Their Majesties were among those who disapproved of my appointment, considering me to be much too young.'[1] A bag of nerves, the governess did her best to make a good impression. When the King and Queen arrived, she was overcome with a profound sense of reverence. Queen Mary smiled at her, while George V merely grunted: 'For the love of God, teach Margaret and Lilibet a decent hand; that is my only request. None of my children can write properly.'[2] Miss Crawford was duly appointed. Known by her protégées as 'Crawfie', she remained with them for seven years.

In London, the Duke and Duchess of York and their daughters lived at 145 Piccadilly, a private mansion near Green Park. They lived modestly, with social gatherings being kept to the bare minimum. Above all, the Yorks enjoyed spending time with their children, and evenings spent reading or chatting around the fireplace. The Duchess was a devoted mother and a careful, thrifty lady of the house; the opposite of a feather-brain. 'She never went in for anything too fashionable,' recalls Crawford. Elizabeth and Margaret's wardrobes would have seemed more at home in a boarding school than in a life of luxury. 'The princesses could not have been dressed more simply. They wore cotton dresses – blue for the most part, their mother's favourite colour – with floral patterns, and various matching cardigans when it was chilly outside.'[3] For everyday life, berets were a staple. When the princesses needed to wear a more sophisticated headpiece, however – especially when they were making a public appearance alongside their parents and grandparents – they would wear straw hats adorned with flowers purchased from Smith & Co., a boutique on Sloane Street. The press went into raptures over these childish variations on their mother's own hats.

THE CALL TO ARMS

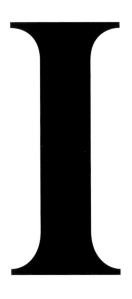n February 1945 Princess Elizabeth, who was nearly 19, joined the Auxiliary Territorial Service (ATS), originally a women's voluntary service set up in 1938, and a separate branch of the British Army from 1941. Despite not fighting on the front, the women of the ATS were a vital cog in the war machine, as cooks, switchboard operators, secretaries, nursing auxiliaries and so on. As the conflict went on, they took over increasingly strategic roles from men, including in the anti-aircraft batteries. In 1945 there were nearly 200,000 of them. Enlisting was far from risk-free, and more than 700 of these women lost their lives. The Princess's decision to join the ATS proved a powerful symbol and an excellent way of remobilising the troops, as is clearly demonstrated by a letter that Leslie Whateley, director of the ATS, sent to Lady Delia Peel, the Queen's lady-in-waiting, on 8 March 1945: 'Words cannot express the effect this has had on morale within the service. It is all our women are talking about. I have been conscious of just how tired many of the women are for some time now; and I've been racking my brains to find a way to inspire them, only too aware of the task that still lies ahead of us.'

The fact that Princess Elizabeth had to implore her parents to allow her to join the ATS only heightened

the effect. Having joined as a junior officer, before being quickly promoted to junior commander, Elizabeth was the first female member of the royal family to sign up to the Armed Forces as a full-time member. During her time in the army, she took her driving test and learned how to read a road map, how to change a tyre and even how to dismantle an engine. Her one privilege was that every evening she could return home to spend the night with her family at Windsor Castle. On all other accounts, she was in the same boat as everyone else, and wore the standard uniform: a khaki wool jacket, a simple skirt in the same colour – or trousers for mechanical work – a blouse, a tie and a service cap bearing the badge of the regiment. Compared to the outfits worn by women in the Royal Navy or the Royal Air Force, the ATS uniform was hardly the stuff of dreams for young women. The cap, in particular, was the subject of many complaints. In 1941, to make it more glamorous, the army resolved to create a more feminine side cap. Those who wished to purchase it had to do so using their own funds: for the price of two pounds sterling for officers, and ten shillings for anyone else. The side cap was a huge success. Elizabeth, for her part, settled for the old model.

In 1949 the ATS was disbanded and absorbed into the Women's Royal Army Corps. The Princess joined. Having initially been appointed Honorary Senior Controller, she was subsequently appointed Honorary Brigadier before she left the army in 1952 to ascend the throne.

A LESSON IN STYLE

Cape Town
April 1947

While the royal family emerged from the war in a blaze of glory, the United Kingdom struggled to recover, despite having come out on the winning side. The economy had been bled dry, the Empire was weakened and the King was exhausted. Despite a staggering lack of funds – or perhaps to divert public attention – the government urged King George VI to agree to a tour of South Africa in 1947. On 31 January the King, Queen and princesses boarded HMS *Vanguard* in Portsmouth. The 16-day crossing proved a delightful break, especially for Elizabeth and Margaret; this was their first journey overseas, and the crew members proved friendly playmates for the two young girls.

With their arrival in Cape Town, however, the break was brought to a sudden close. The South Africa tour proved a particularly tricky affair, with racial tension growing increasingly fraught in the country. Duty-bound to maintain a position of strict neutrality, George VI did his best to put on a good show. Behind the scenes, however, the King was appalled at not being able to decorate the people of colour who had distinguished themselves during the war. He was only just permitted to attend a large Zulu gathering – the first in 60 years – during which nearly 80,000 people gathered in the town of Eshowe.

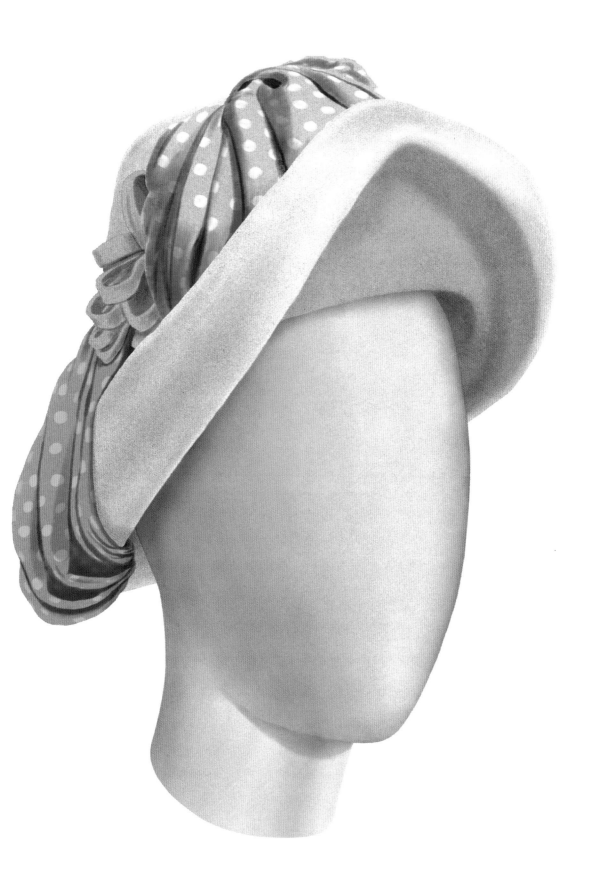

Despite several calls for a boycott, the South Africans extended a warm welcome to the royal family. George VI's wife, Queen Elizabeth, worked wonders. In Durban, a multiracial crowd cried out: 'We love you, Queen!'[4] She certainly did not cut any corners; an entire carriage of the Windsors' train was dedicated to her and her daughters' wardrobes. In charge of her hats, as well, for the first time, as those of the princesses, the milliner Aage Thaarup indulged his passion for ostrich feathers, a speciality of South Africa that was all the rage in London. For the two princesses, he focused on ribbons and tulle, which were mainly used to adorn light straw headpieces: 'Everyone had had enough of the gloominess and austerity of the war. I wanted to make hats that were truly uplifting and appealing.'[5] He was nonetheless concerned by both the humidity of the climate, which he believed to be capable of rusting the smallest pin, and the local insects, which he seemed to think were about to devour his masterpieces.

More than just a lesson in style, however, the South Africa tour marked the future Elizabeth II's first steps in the world of diplomacy. On 21 April, her twenty-first birthday, the young woman addressed the nation via the BBC. From Cape Town, she solemnly declared that she would dedicate her entire life to the 'great family of the Commonwealth'. Deep down, however, Elizabeth was primarily focused on preparing to start her own family. Upon her return from South Africa, on 10 July 1947, Buckingham Palace announced the heir to the throne's engagement to Lieutenant Philip Mountbatten. They celebrated their marriage in London on 20 November that year.

Cape Town   April 1947

A PRINCESS IN PARIS

L yon silks, a sports car, a case of Camembert, a miniature Eiffel Tower made of gold and diamonds … Before they had even arrived, the British Embassy in Paris was being showered with the most extravagant gifts. In the spring of 1948 Elizabeth and Philip were expected in the French capital for an official five-day visit, the Princess's first tour outside the British Empire. On the morning of Saturday 15 May, the people of Paris were filled with anticipation. 'Over an hour before the royal train was due to arrive, young men and women were already gathered in large numbers behind the white barriers surrounding the main courtyard of Gare du Nord,' recounted a correspondent for the daily newspaper *France-Soir*. While starry-eyed girls could not fail to be charmed by the Duke of Edinburgh's good looks, it was the young British princess whom people were most eager to see: 'She appeared at the door smiling, wearing a grey hat decorated with roses, and received Paris's first respects in the form of a "hurrah" proclaimed by thousands.'[6] The young couple did not hang around, however, quickly dashing off to the Elysée Palace, where they were expected by President Vincent Auriol and his wife, Michelle.

What would the future queen wear during those five days? Would she follow the 'New Look'? The

34
—
35

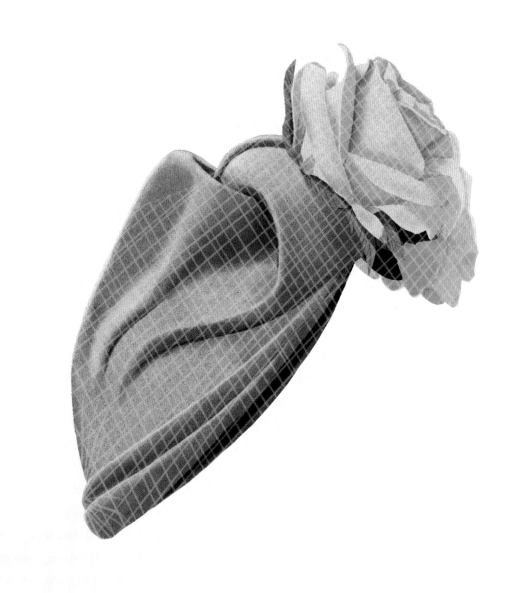

Windsors are not known for starting fashions; they only follow them at a push. Ten years earlier, during George VI and his wife's visit in 1938, the dressmaker Norman Hartnell designed white crinoline dresses for the Queen, going completely against the taste of the time. She was in mourning for her mother, the Countess of Strathmore, who had passed away three weeks earlier, and white was chosen over black. For their daughter's trip, the same designer prepared a series of elegant but by no means ground-breaking ensembles: 'As usual, the princess merely hinted at the "New Look": her hems were a little too long, her skirts a bit too full, and her heels a bit too high.'[7]

Fortunately, the Princess's hats were enough to sustain the conversation during the dinners in town. The press did their best to unlock their secrets. Even the communist daily *Ce Soir* played along: 'She has seven new hats to choose from, made by the Danish milliner Aage Thaarup: two felt hats (one white and one aquamarine, the latter in the Napoleonic style), and five straw hats, charmingly decorated with tulle, organdie, sprigs of white heather and foam. They are all worn tilted to one side, and two of them are accompanied by matching gauntlet gloves.'[8]

As she waved to the crowds from the grandstand at Longchamp Racecourse or from the shuttle named in her honour for a cruise along the Seine, the Princess was impeccably hatted. At the Palais Galliera, she triumphed. Invited to open the exhibition 'Huit siècles de vie britannique à Paris' ('Eight centuries of British life in Paris'), she delivered her speech in perfect French under the admiring gaze of the President of the Municipal Council, Pierre de Gaulle: 'I have wanted to come to France for a long time. My parents' memories of their frequent trips to your beautiful country have only made me more impatient to visit Paris. I cannot put into words how overjoyed I am finally to be here among you.'

Paris   15 May 1948

TROOPING THE COLOUR

H is Majesty needed to rest. While his cousin King Haakon VII of Norway was visiting the United Kingdom, George VI cancelled his engagements for the next four weeks, notably his attendance of Trooping the Colour, the ceremony held to mark his official birthday. The announcement was made on the evening of 4 June 1951, just three days before the event, and the news hit the headlines the following day. 'Although his overall condition has improved, the inflammation in His Majesty's lung has not completely disappeared,' the papers reported. The reality was far more serious than Buckingham Palace wished to admit, however. Worn out by years of war and heavy smoking, King George was dying of an unidentified cancer. Three months later, in September 1951, a board of doctors concluded that one of his lungs should be removed. The medical reports were presented in such a way as to hide the gravity of the situation from the public, however.

In the meantime, a replacement needed to be found for the King, and Princess Elizabeth was asked to represent her father at the military parade. Buckingham Palace had been preparing for such an eventuality for several months. This is clearly evidenced by the discreet preparations, in which Aage Thaarup had played his part: 'One morning

in the spring of 1950, I was called to Buckingham Palace. The Queen, then Princess Elizabeth, was to replace King George at Trooping the Colour. The princess had to wear her colonel-in-chief uniform, with a split skirt so she could ride side-saddle.'[9] What hat would confer a suitable gravity upon the heir to the throne? The King and princes were required to wear a black bearskin hat dating back to Napoleon's grenadiers. What about a 25-year-old woman, though? At the War Office, they stuck to their guns: it was the bearskin hat or nothing! Negotiations got underway. Might a less high, and thus less heavy, hat be conceivable? However hardy Princess Elizabeth was, the royal family were determined to spare her. The heat under such a towering headpiece could easily make her feel unwell, and a fainting spell was to be avoided at all costs. Thaarup was charged with finding a compromise: 'It needed to be dignified, elegant and military.'[10] The milliner turned to France for inspiration. In Paris, the tricorn hat seemed to present the ideal solution. Worn by soldiers since the end of the 17th century, it became such a popular fashion accessory under Louis XV that it was even worn by women during the hunting season.

Back in London, Thaarup proposed his idea, which received everyone's approval, notably that of the Princess herself. Without any adornment, however, the headpiece looked a little sorry for itself. Lord Mountbatten, Prince Philip's uncle, therefore proposed adding a feather that one of his ancestors had worn on the battlefield – no one knew which ancestor, or which battle. Thaarup believed a more modest feather would be preferable. The results speak for themselves: on 7 June 1951 Princess Elizabeth cut a fine figure as she inspected the troops in her father's place. She kept her tricorn hat until 1986, changing the feather depending on the regiment being honoured. After that date, she wore civilian clothes and a lady's hat when she attended Trooping the Colour each year.

London   7 June 1951

MORE HATS FOR MISS DONALD

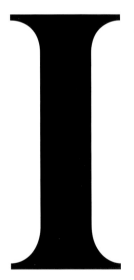

In November 1953, just five months after her coronation at Westminster Abbey, Elizabeth II set off on her first royal tour. The tour was to last six months – she would be accompanied by Prince Philip but not their young children, Charles and Anne – and would cover Bermuda, Jamaica, the Fiji Islands, New Zealand, Australia, Ceylon (now Sri Lanka), Uganda, Malta and Gibraltar. Travelling with 12 tonnes of luggage, the couple wended their way along this winding route, one of the most ambitious communications operations of the Queen's early reign. To open the Australian parliament, Elizabeth even brought her coronation gown with her, designed by Norman Hartnell. Hartnell was given the task of freshening up the Queen's wardrobe, and the milliner Aage Thaarup also got back to work.

Unsurprisingly, the crowning achievement of this first royal tour came in Australia. On 3 February 1954, in blazing sunshine – it was summer in the southern hemisphere – Sydney welcomed its sovereign for the first time in its history. A million onlookers gathered in the streets to watch the Queen pass by; at the time, the city had 1.8 million inhabitants. For eight weeks Philip and Elizabeth travelled across the country, visiting no fewer than 57 towns. For Hartnell and Thaarup, the

tour generated a colossal amount of publicity. What is more, women's magazines had not anticipated that the Queen would wear dresses and hats especially designed for the Australian leg of the tour, and readers of *Woman's Day* were still gushing over the outfits she had debuted in Bermuda two months earlier. Small, brightly coloured hats were in fashion at the time; turquoise and parrot green were particularly popular, as were egret feathers.

A globetrotter at heart, Thaarup happened to be in Australia at the time. This was not the Danish milliner's first trip. Aware of the incredible possibilities of the market there, he had opened a studio and boutique in Sydney, where he landed just a few days before the Queen and the Duke. No sooner had he arrived than the Governor-General of New Zealand – where the royal couple were at the time – contacted him. Against all odds, the Queen did not have enough hats! Would Thaarup come to Her Majesty's assistance, without delay and with the utmost discretion? He sharpened his pencils and set his studio in motion. Conscious of the risk of indiscretion, however, particularly by his employees, the ingenious milliner placed the order under the name 'Miss Donald'. His staff were astonished; who was this mysterious Miss Donald, whom no one had ever laid eyes on? The mystery went unsolved. When the Queen landed in Sydney wearing one of the models they had created in such haste, the saleswomen and workers were taken aback. For, while they could clearly see that this was the hat designed for Miss Donald, they did not guess the trick that had been played on them. Instead, they were outraged; as far as they could tell, Thaarup had copied the Queen's hats for a common client. Shocking!

Canberra   17 February 1954

THE NEW YORK MARATHON

W hat hat would Elizabeth II wear to win over America? While she had stolen the show in France a few months earlier wearing berets designed by Kate Day and Claude Saint-Cyr, turbans were the order of the day for her tour of Canada and the United States. The Queen had taken off from London wearing a velvet turban, and it was sporting another turban – this time in chestnut satin – that she embarked on the last leg of her journey: New York.

At 10 a.m. on 21 October 1957, Elizabeth II and Prince Philip's train arrived at Staten Island, having set off from Washington the evening before. Therein began a fourteen-hour marathon with no fewer than ten engagements on the agenda. First, the royal couple was treated to the traditional ticker-tape parade on Broadway; armed with copious amounts of confetti, New Yorkers gave them a hero's welcome. Elizabeth and Philip then enjoyed luncheon at City Hall with Robert Wagner, mayor of New York, before making their way to the United Nations Headquarters on the bank of the East River. The Queen delivered her first address to the General Assembly – she would not give another until 2010. The flames from the Suez Crisis were still burning, but even the representatives of the Soviet Union and of Egypt attended, although they

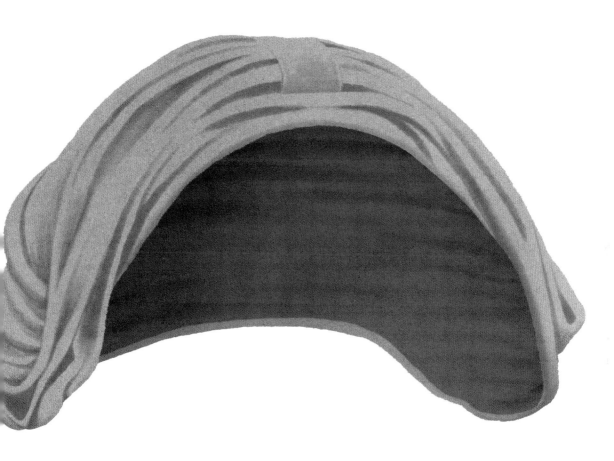

remained silent. The Queen's contribution, which lasted ten minutes exactly, received warm applause. The United Kingdom had, of course, begun the process of decolonisation, embarking upon an 'impressive timetable of liberation', as *Life* magazine had declared in June. 'What vast changes there have been,' its editorial said, since George VI's visit in 1939. 'Since World War II … Britain herself gave independence to 507 million people': in India, Pakistan, Burma (now Myanmar), Sudan, Ghana and Malaysia. 'Elizabeth may properly be known to posterity as the Queen of Independence.'[11]

The rest of the programme was comparatively light, being dedicated to tourist activities and, notably, climbing the Empire State Building, the highest building in the world at the time. The authorities even recruited a former London bobby to serve as a luxury bellboy. Two American agents were employed to keep an eye on the elevator machinery in the basement, however. In total, 5,000 soldiers and policemen were deployed for the day. The Windsors were showered with gifts. Queen Elizabeth received a gold-plated miniature Empire State Building with an antenna adorned with rubies, and Prince Philip received a cigarette holder. Their children did not go empty-handed, either; there was a key ring for Prince Charles, and a bracelet for Princess Anne. That evening, the Queen and the Duke of Edinburgh were invited to a gala dinner put on by the British community of New York, followed by a ball on Park Avenue in honour of the Commonwealth. They made only a fleeting appearance, however, since their plane was due to take off at 12.45 a.m. 'We have but one regret; that we must leave so soon,' declared the Queen.[12]

New York   21 October 1957

MARGARET GETS MARRIED

'You look after your Empire and I'll look after my life,' Princess Margaret once famously snapped at the Queen after being reprimanded by her sister for flirting. Did this really happen? It easily could have. It is a sufficiently saucy remark – and indicative of the image left by Elizabeth II's younger sister – to have been passed down for posterity. Margaret, known as the 'Rebel Royal', devastated by her impossible love for Group Captain Peter Townsend, a divorcé 15 years her senior, picked herself up again. On 6 May 1960 Elizabeth could finally breathe a sigh of relief: the princess had found her match in Antony Armstrong-Jones, known as Tony, a brilliant, nonchalant fashion photographer. What did it matter if Margaret was the first member of the British royal family to marry a commoner in 400 years? She would also be the first to get divorced since Henry VIII …

In May that year, London was jubilant. The ceremony, held in Westminster Abbey, was the first royal wedding to be broadcast on television. Crowds filled the streets once again. Norman Hartnell designed not only the bride's gown but also the outfits worn by the Queen Mother, the Duchess of Kent and, of course, Queen Elizabeth herself. For the sovereign, the indefatigable dressmaker proposed a turquoise dress with matching

WHEN I LOOK AT PHOTOGRAPHS OF THE QUEEN THESE DAYS, I THINK, WITHOUT MODESTY, HOW PRETTY THE CLOTHES I MADE FOR HER WERE.

Claude Saint-Cyr

bolero. The journalists who were lucky enough to see the sketches before the big day went into raptures over the hat: 'a headdress featuring two large blue roses, decorated with velvet leaves and a turquoise veil'. The *Daily Mirror* saw the funny side of a day on which 'the Queen, wearing her little hat, lets the bride carry the crown alone for once.' It was actually a tiara, which Margaret had purchased herself a few months before the ceremony: another quirk.

So that she would be taller than her sister, Margaret, who was even shorter than Elizabeth – 5ft 1in compared to 5ft 3in – opted for a raised bun, created by Claude Saint-Cyr, who was also well known for her hairdressing talent. Saint-Cyr later described what went on behind the scenes at the ceremony: 'I went to see Margaret at her residence and Tony at his. I had bumped into him before at the *Vogue* studios, so I already knew him a little. He had very specific ideas about what he wanted; he wanted his wife to be dressed like a communicant. He must have been sick and tired of fripperies. Margaret, for her part, did me a big favour by choosing an articulated tiara, which was easy to put on and fasten in place.'[13]

As sisters, Margaret and Elizabeth were close yet nothing alike. This can even be seen in their hats, and the way they wore them. 'The Queen and her sister were nothing like one another,' recalls Saint-Cyr. 'They were both beautiful, but while one knew how to pose, the other did not. Naturally coquettish, Margaret knew which was her good side, how to place one foot forward, how to elongate her neck; in short, how to present herself to her best advantage when she was being photographed. The Queen, however, had no idea. She did not come alive in front of the lens, nor would she pose; she simply contented herself with being Queen.'[14]

London   6 May 1960

THE CHARM AFTER THE STORM

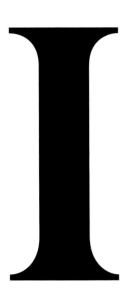

It was 11.37 a.m. on the dot. On 1 February 1961, while on a six-week tour of the Indian subcontinent, Elizabeth II set foot on Pakistani soil for the very first time. Buttoned up in his uniform, President Muhammad Ayub Khan was waiting on the airport tarmac, not for the sovereign, but for his 'guest'. The nuance is by no means simply anecdotal: having been independent since 1947, Pakistan was determined to demonstrate that it had put the British Empire behind it.

This did not stop the people of Karachi from extending a warm welcome to the Queen, however. For her part, she spared no effort to do credit to them, which can be seen as much in her choice of clothing as in her words. On that first day, she wore a new dress designed by Norman Hartnell, made in an incredible Shantung silk with bronze hues. Claude Saint-Cyr had made her a hat adorned with petals and feathers, in the same golden shades. The Queen fitted in perfectly; she was surrounded by women decked out in jewellery and wearing the *shalwar kameez* – the national costume – which was also presented to her as a gift. To Pakistani women's even greater delight, the government had decided, on the Queen's behalf, to relax a law introduced two years earlier that prohibited receptions involving more than 35 people (weddings in Pakistan can have up to 2,000 guests).

Thanks to Elizabeth and Philip, garden parties were revived. On average, it rains for only six days a year in Karachi, but as luck would have it, a violent storm broke out during a cocktail reception at the residence of the High Commissioner for the Commonwealth. The poles of one of the tents gave way, crashing down in a terrible din on to 200 guests who were waiting for the royal couple. The staff rushed to the tent – or what remained of it – and tore at the canvas with knives, releasing the wretched guests, who were stunned and soaking wet. Other, more fortunate souls looked on from the High Commissioner's residence, where they had taken refuge. Luckily, no one was injured. When the Queen and the Duke of Edinburgh arrived, the crowd had picked itself up again. 'I always feel I take the rain with me, but it has never been this catastrophic before,' announced Elizabeth, truly devastated.[15]

As vast as the High Commissioner's property was, it could house the 2,000 guests only at a pinch, especially since water was coming in on all sides there too. The couple wove their way through, assisted by servants shouting 'Mind out the way!' every few steps. Crammed together in the reception rooms, the women who were not on the Queen's pathway took out their compact mirrors to try to catch sight of her. The sun finally came out again, and the crowd went back out on to the soaked lawns, in high spirits once again. As on the balcony of Buckingham Palace, Elizabeth and Philip waved to the crowd from one of the terraces. The storm was already no more than a distant memory.

Karachi   1 February 1961

FLOWER POWER

'The Queen has chosen the flowers!'[16] The British press passed the word around, and their readers understood: in the early 1960s women, including Elizabeth II herself, were wearing flowers around their heads, and they would continue to do so for a decade. The trend made fortunes for florists selling artificial flowers, while their direct competitors – those who dealt in ornamental plumes and feathers – looked on in dismay. With hairdressers beginning to overshadow them, milliners saw this as an opportunity to reinvent themselves. When choosing between a new hat and a new haircut, the young generation did not hesitate. At Buckingham Palace, however, Aage Thaarup was still running the show. Jill Carey, a journalist for the *Coventry Evening Telegraph*, raved about the milliner's latest creations, which he presented in London in January 1960. 'Aage Thaarup has gone for flowers. One of his boaters is made with dandelions, the flowers he presented in England during his first collection before the war. He also uses roses, making a cocktail hat out of yellow rose petals.
It's his silk hats that are making headlines, however. They are bright and cheerful but also a sophisticated choice for women over thirty. They are made with organza in soft pastel colours.'[17]

The following year, petal hats were all the rage.

Since her tour of India and Pakistan in February, Elizabeth II seemed to have been collecting them. On 31 May 1961 she wore a petal hat for one of Britain's most famous horse races: the Epsom Derby. This was a historic moment: for the first time in 182 years, the first three horses to cross the finishing line were owned by women. One month later, Her Majesty's petals worked wonders once again at Royal Ascot. 'The Queen seems particularly partial to hats adorned with flowers and petals. I imagine everyone has seen the pretty hat she wore for the opening of Ascot on the television or in photographs in the newspapers. It was in the palest duck-egg blue. It went perfectly with her wild silk dress and coat and had most of the women there feeling envious. Another day, the Queen also opted for a petal hat, this time in yellow hues,' recounted a fashion journalist at the time.[18]

Simone Mirman established herself as the master of these hats adorned with petals and little flowers. 'The prettiest hats are the ones designed by Simone Mirman for Princess Margaret,' another journalist reported. 'Many are covered with tiny flowers – usually a sort of hybrid daisy – and there is also a model made from a complete bunch of summer flowers on an almost invisible base.'[19] The hat (generally in the cloche style) is hidden from view under corollas, bunches of hydrangeas and lilies.

THE SPAGHETTI HAT

'The Queen's hats are still the talk of the town among women in West Germany.' On 2 July 1965 the *Marylebone Mercury* – one of London's longest-standing newspapers – was sure of it: with her fascinators, Elizabeth II had just treated the Federal Republic of Germany to a lesson in style and optimism. 'Her Majesty's exquisite taste has proved a fantastic boost for the country's milliners,' the paper raved. As for her hats, perhaps most memorable of all was Simone Mirman's incredible invention, christened the 'spaghetti hat'. The milliner's daughter Sophie Mirman remembers it to this day: 'It was made of small ribbons cut into a piece of organza. It took a ridiculous amount of time to make, requiring the utmost dexterity.'[20]

Queen Elizabeth had not come to Germany to be a fashion icon, however. It was the first time in 52 years that a British sovereign had gone to Berlin. George V, the last to do so, visited in 1913 at the invitation of his cousin Emperor Wilhelm II, just a few months before the start of the First World War. In 1917 Elizabeth II's grandfather had resolved to cover up the Germanic origins of his family by changing the name of the dynasty: the Saxe-Coburg-Gothas became the Windsors, after the castle of the same name. He also prohibited his family from using the titles of Duke and Duchess of Saxe. The ties with

66
—
67

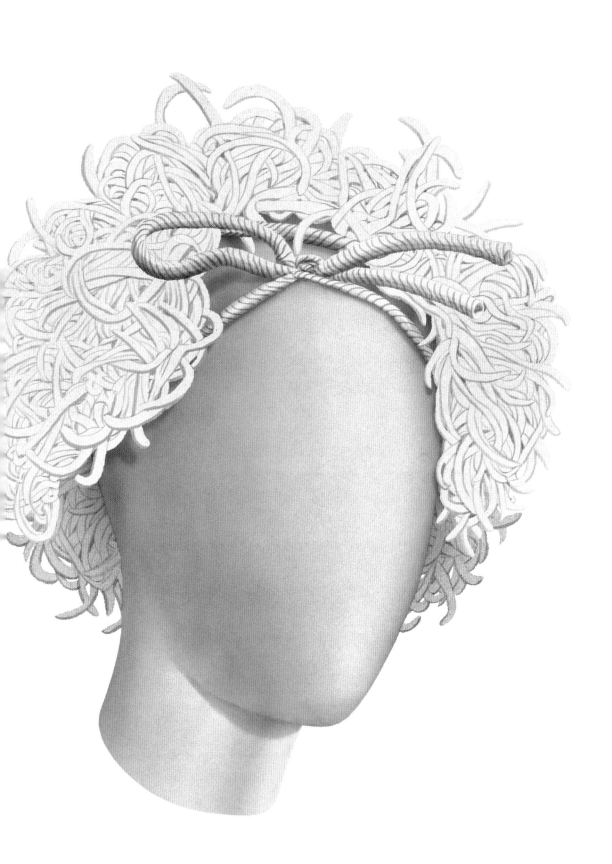

Germany were severed. Edward VIII's contact with the Third Reich – the Duke of Windsor and his wife met Adolf Hitler and several Nazi officials in 1937 – tarnished the royal family for a long time. In 1947 not one of Philip Mountbatten's sisters – all of whom were married to German princes – was invited to his wedding to Princess Elizabeth.

On 27 May 1965, after nine days in the Federal Republic of Germany, the Queen flew over the Republic in an uneventful journey. In West Berlin, she was greeted by 100,000 people. The people of East Germany, on the other hand, made a point of ignoring her trip. Officially, the Queen's arrival in Berlin was a non-event. On the other side of the wall, however, the public were far more curious than the authorities cared to admit. The East German police had to disperse several hundred onlookers trying to catch sight of Elizabeth at Brandenburg Gate.

Behind closed doors, people in East Berlin turned on their television sets to watch the West German 'propaganda', and saw the Queen's spaghetti hat for themselves. They were better served than their British counterparts. On BBC1, the special programme *The Queen in Germany*, broadcast live from Berlin, came up against one technical problem after another. Realising that he had been commentating on the event with no image for more than half an hour, the star journalist Richard Dimbleby exclaimed 'Sweet Jesus!', before pulling himself together and starting his lengthy monologue again. It was, by his own admission, his worst gaffe in his 30-year career to date.

Berlin

27 May 1965

UNCLE DICKIE

t the age of 65, Louis Mountbatten – Count of Burma and the Last Viceroy of India – retired from the Royal Navy. Admiral of the Fleet since 1956 and then Chief of the Defence Staff of the Armed Forces, Uncle Dickie – as he was known affectionately within the family – was a living legend. He was not the sort of man to withdraw completely from affairs. On 26 July 1965, just two weeks after he had cleared his desk and been awarded full military honours, he was appointed Governor of the Isle of Wight by the Queen. The event also provided Elizabeth with an opportunity to visit the island, a popular destination for holidaymakers. Met with great fanfare in Newport, the island's principal town, the Queen and the Duke of Edinburgh set off to visit Osborne House, a place dearly loved by Queen Victoria, Elizabeth's great-great-grandmother and Lord Mountbatten's great-grandmother. It had been a frequent holiday destination for Victoria, and it was there that she passed away in 1901.

The main event of Elizabeth's visit, however, was without doubt the ceremony held to install the new governor at Carisbrooke Castle, a former official royal residence. Lord Mountbatten, the sixty-eighth person to take the role, greeted the Queen with a kiss on the hand. 'Your Majesty, my honour at being appointed

Governor of the Isle of Wight is rendered even greater by your decision to preside over the ceremony in person,' said her kindly uncle. The sovereign, who was wearing a coral hat, certainly owed him that. She was in excellent spirits, and a jovial atmosphere prevailed over the island on that midsummer's day, much like that of a village fair.

Even Prince Philip's gaffes could not spoil the celebrations. When the couple arrived at the town hall, the Duke of Edinburgh was taken aback by the state of the councillors' clothing, declaring it to be 'a little on the shabby side'. The comment was met with amusement for the most part, but mortified the poor councillors themselves. 'The council is planning to replace them. There has been a great deal of discussion about the matter,' one of them said in their defence. 'That wouldn't be a bad idea,' Philip responded sarcastically, deriving far more enjoyment from the beauty pageants held that afternoon than from the morning's formal honours.[21]

When the time came for the royal visitors to leave the island, one final surprise awaited them. Rather than taking the royal barge, which was expected to transport them back to the yacht *Britannia*, Elizabeth and Philip were invited to board one of the very first hovercraft intended for the general public; a symbol of triumphant progress. Lord Mountbatten watched from port as the vessel made its thunderous departure. After just 300 m (330 yd), however, it began to judder dangerously. The air bags quickly deflated and the hovercraft packed up. The vessel had to be towed back, to 'save' the Queen and the Prince Consort. Elizabeth did her best to console the crew, who were visibly put out. 'If it were a plane, Prince Charles would already be on the throne,' proclaimed Lord Mountbatten philosophically.[22]

Isle of Wight   26 July 1965

CROWNING CHARLES

O n 1 July 1969, at Caernarfon Castle, Charles knelt before the Queen. Wearing his Colonel-in-Chief uniform for the Royal Regiment of Wales, the young man – aged 20 – was about to be officially appointed Prince of Wales, in front of 4,000 guests and 500 million television viewers. The grand ceremony was designed by his uncle Antony Armstrong-Jones, who had held the title of Count of Snowdon since his marriage to Princess Margaret. The Duke of Norfolk remained the official master of ceremonies, however, as had been the case for coronations and royal funerals since 1386. A skilled professional, Lord Snowdon was determined to go all out. Such was his attention to detail that each of the 4,000 chairs reserved for the public was covered in Welsh tweed, and convex mirrors were installed so that all guests could follow every detail of the ceremony, wherever they were seated. The skilled director designed a circular slate platform in the centre of the courtyard, protected by a Plexiglas canopy, where the participants could take their places. The spectacle certainly lived up to expectation, resembling a scene of medieval phantasmagoria as much as the futurist aesthetic of the 1960s.

The investiture was not new, however; the last such ceremony had taken place on 13 July 1911, also at Caernarfon Castle. On that day, the future Edward

VIII (later the Duke of Windsor) was crowned Prince of Wales by his father, George V, at the age of just 17 – a crown he made sure to take with him after his abdication in 1936. Unable to demand the return of the precious object, Buckingham Palace was forced to order a new one. The task of creating Charles's crown was entrusted to the goldsmith and architect Louis Osman. He designed a modern, light object adorned with emeralds and 13 diamonds arranged in the shape of the Scorpio constellation, the prince's star sign. An actual ping-pong ball, plated in gold, sits on top.

This crown was not the only one to pique the public's interest, however. Would the Queen wear her own crown for the investiture? Elizabeth opted instead for a hat, and Simone Mirman was charged with making it. She came up with a silk headpiece embroidered with pearls, loosely inspired by headdresses from the Tudor period: yet another historical reference in a setting already laden with symbolism.

While the letters patent – conferring the titles, honours and privileges of the Principality of Wales and of the Earldom of Chester on the heir to the throne – were being read out in Welsh, Elizabeth handed Charles the sword, ring, sceptre, and velvet and ermine cloak. 'I, Charles, Prince of Wales, do become your liege man': the prince made his oath to his mother before being cheered by the crowd. The Windsors could relax; Charles had proved to be up to the task. Most importantly, however, the celebration had not been disturbed by Welsh separatists, even though that same morning two such men had been killed after the explosion of a home-made bomb intended for the royal family.

Caernarfon   1 July 1969

ONE STEP CLOSER TO THE PUBLIC

Sixteen years had passed since Queen Elizabeth and Prince Philip's first visit to Australia. Since the royal tour of 1954, the Australians had had the opportunity to get to know this royal family from the other side of the world, which was also their own. Between 1954 and 1970 Prince Philip himself had visited the island on five occasions: once with the Queen, in 1963, and four times on his own, in 1956, 1962, 1965 and 1968. Another tour of Oceania took place in March 1970, the bicentenary of Captain James Cook's first expedition.

How could the sacred fire be kept alight, however? Buckingham Palace was conscious of the fact that the Queen was no longer the glamorous figure who had inspired women back in the 1950s. As a mother of four – including two young adults – she was in the prime of life, a reassuring figure, to be sure, but a conservative one to say the least, at a time when the public was crying out for modernity and human warmth.

It was actually an Australian, William Heseltine, who helped the Windsors to present a more likeable face to the world. A native of the small town of York on the outskirts of Perth, Western Australia, Heseltine, who had settled in England, was in charge of public relations for Her Majesty. The previous year he had outdone himself by opening up the royal palaces to the

78
—
79

I THINK SHE WEARS WHAT SHE LIKES BUT THAT SHE ALSO LIKES TO PLEAS THE PUBLIC.

Simone Mirman

cameras of the BBC, which was granted permission to film the royal family in private for almost a year. The programme was initially intended to take the form of a less ambitious documentary about the heir to the throne, but Heseltine was set on going big, as the director Richard Cawston explained in 1971: 'In the end, we decided that it would not be a film about Prince Charles, but rather about the task that lay ahead of him. The only way to reveal it in its full extent was to show the work carried out by the Queen herself.'[23] Called *Royal Family*, the documentary was a huge success, with the first broadcast attracting an audience of no fewer than 40 million. Viewers watched incredulously as Prince Philip and Princess Anne grilled sausages at Balmoral and the Queen went into a grocery shop to buy an ice cream for the newest member of the family, Prince Edward. The Windsors were finally sharing their private lives, even if they did later regret it: the BBC was politely asked never to broadcast the film again.

Be that as it may, modernisation was underway, and there was no stopping it now. For the tour in 1970, the Queen placed an order for 56 dresses from her dressmakers Norman Hartnell and Hardy Amies, who were then asked to shorten them. 'As short as is permitted', Amies noted on a photograph of the Queen; he loathed miniskirts. To make the outfits, the designer teamed up with the young milliner Frederick Fox, who was also Australian. It was, however, Simone Mirman who came up with the little beret covered with ivory silk ribbons that the Queen wore on 1 May 1970 for one of her very first walkabouts – Heseltine's latest innovation. Accustomed to mixing only with the elite, Elizabeth nevertheless came around to the idea and broke a century-long monarchical tradition by walking up and down streets packed with people. For the first time ever, she went out to meet the public in person – to their great delight.

Sydney   1 May 1970

THE DUKE OF WINDSOR QUIETLY PASSES AWAY

'Splendid!', the *Daily Mirror* declared proudly of its sovereign on 16 May 1972. 'The Queen changed her outfit five times in seven hours yesterday, treating Paris to a spectacular royal fashion display.' While officially the state visit to France in May 1972 had got off to an excellent start – with a dinner at the Grand Trianon and a ballet at the Royal Opera of Versailles – the atmosphere behind the scenes was more sombre. The reason was the poor health of the Duke of Windsor, the former King Edward VIII, who was suffering from cancer of the throat. Living in a private mansion on the edge of the Bois de Boulogne with his wife, Wallis Simpson, Elizabeth's uncle had been a thorn in the family's side since his abdication in 1936, although tension had gradually begun to wane. In 1967 the Queen invited him and, exceptionally, his wife to the inauguration of a commemorative plaque for Queen Mary, his mother, who had spent her whole life refusing to meet Wallis. The Duke and Duchess were hoping for a return to grace, and the Duchess hoped she might finally be granted the right to use the long-coveted title of Her Royal Highness. Alas, it was not to be. Vexed at once again being invited to attend his grand-nephew's investiture as Prince of Wales in 1969 alone, the Duke made his excuses and contented himself with watching the event on television, as he had his niece's coronation

82
—
83

YOU CAN BE ANYONE YOU WANT TO BE WITH A HAT.

Frederick Fox

in 1953. The former sovereign's health was gradually deteriorating. Having been admitted to the American Hospital in Neuilly-sur-Seine in February 1972, he was a shadow of his normal self when he returned home.

What if he passed away in the middle of the state visit? 'Politically, it would be a disaster,' the British Ambassador to Paris, Sir Christopher Soames said in despair.[24] 'I know he is dying; you know he is dying; but officially we don't know anything,' the Queen's private secretary, Martin Charteris, told a royal reporter.[25] Buckingham Palace was walking on eggshells.

It was decided that the Queen's agenda would include one last interview with her uncle. On 18 May she, Prince Philip and Prince Charles were at Longchamp Racecourse. Wearing a blue patterned coat designed by Hardy Amies, and a fine straw Breton hat, the Queen was enjoying the races. The royal family was expected for tea with the Windsors, however, who lived very close by. When she welcomed her guests on the steps, Wallis put on a display of the utmost reverence, which she had resolutely refrained from doing in 1967, when faced with her lifelong rival the Queen Mother. For her, a firm handshake was as far as she would go. She was no doubt touched by the attention extended to her husband. In the sitting room, the Duchess served tea for the Queen, the Duke of Edinburgh and their son. The former king was unable to leave his bedroom. He nonetheless insisted on getting dressed and sitting in an armchair to receive his niece, who alone was permitted to visit him upstairs. What did they say to each other during this final quarter of an hour alone together? No one will ever know. The Queen left France the following day. The Duke of Windsor – the former King of Great Britain, Ireland and the British Dominions, and former Emperor of India – passed away nine days later.

Paris   18 May 1972

HIGHCLERE

E lizabeth II's passion for corgis is legendary, but the Queen was also passionate about horses, an excellent rider and an unparalleled breeder, as her great-grandfather Edward VII had been. Edward was the first sovereign to win the Epsom Derby in 1909. It was with her grandfather George V, however, that little Lilibet took her first steps in the field. Not exactly renowned for his patience with children, particularly his own, the elderly king was nonetheless found one day crawling along the floor in front of his granddaughter, whinnying away. The little girl cheered him on in delight. For her fourth birthday, George gave the future Elizabeth II her first Shetland pony, called Peggy.

For the Queen, horses were a refuge. She had up to 30 in training on her estate at Sandringham, as well as on stud farms in Kentucky. Her champions did her proud, distinguishing themselves in the United Kingdom and overseas. It was in 1974 in Chantilly, France, however, that the Queen carried off one of her greatest victories, when her filly Highclere won the Prix de Diane. That day, the sovereign arrived at the racecourse in a convertible, to great applause. Her incredible green hat is emblematic of Simone Mirman's style at the time, inspired by the bouffant hairstyles of the 1960s and 1970s.

Elizabeth watched from the official gallery as her filly carried off her great victory, amid scenes of jubilation. The journalist Léon Zitrone described the race: 'Three hundred metres from the post, when Highclere took the lead, the Queen made an extraordinary gesture; she raised her left hand to her lips to stop herself from crying out in joy. On the screen, it was clear how delighted she was, however, and when I saw her smile I took the liberty of shouting into the microphone: "The English are not impassive!"'[26]

The Queen was presented with the cup by the organisers, who tried to take it back so that they could have it engraved with her and her filly's names, as was standard practice. The sovereign refused outright, however, resolved to return with it to Windsor Castle that evening for a banquet with her nearest and dearest, whom she had invited to celebrate the great success. Louis Romanent, President of the International Federation of Horse-Racing Authorities, who was present that day, shared the following anecdote with the journalist Isabelle Rivère 40 years later: '"Don't worry," the Queen smiled in front of the officials, who were clearly put out. "We have excellent engravers in England!"'[27]

Horse racing, and especially the races at Ascot, remained a source of great joy for the Queen throughout her life. In 2020, during the Covid-19 pandemic, the competition took place with no audience for the first time ever, and thus also in Elizabeth II's absence. In 68 years, this was a first. As well as the races, the Queen loved riding, and she had several faithful companions during her reign. For 18 years her horse Burmese – a gift from the Royal Canadian Mounted Police – had the great honour of being her mount for the Trooping the Colour ceremony, held in London every year to celebrate her birthday. At the age of 96, she had lost none of her bravura, even if in her final days it was a pony, Balmoral Fern, that had the privilege of carrying Her Majesty out on the Windsor estate on fine days.

Chantilly   16 June 1974

THE CHRYSANTHEMUM THRONE

'My dearest Mama,' Prince Alfred wrote on 3 September 1869 to his mother, Queen Elizabeth, from Edo (later Tokyo). 'I feel quite at a loss. Every thing is so new & so quaint that I am quite bewildered.' After more than two centuries of self-isolation, Japan had opened up to the world once again. Alfred was the first European prince to discover this incredible empire, which had always been a source of fascination for Westerners and whose lacquerware and china they had been snapping up since the 18th century. In 1881 it was the turn of his nephews – the Prince of Wales's eldest sons – to visit the archipelago. Albert Victor and George were 18 and 16 years old, respectively. The visit made such an impression on them that they decided to get themselves tattooed: Albert Victor chose an image of a pair of storks, a symbol of longevity and good fortune – he died of pneumonia at the age of 28 – and George, the future George V, the Queen's grandfather, got a dragon and a tiger, representing the coming together of East and West.

While the British royal family and the imperial family of Japan had been on good terms before the crisis of 1929 – Crown Prince Hirohito visited the United Kingdom in 1921, and the future Edward VIII visited Japan in 1922 – the nationalism of the 1930s and Japan's expansionist ambitions cast the Chrysanthemum

Throne firmly in the enemy camp. It was not until the Queen's coronation in 1953, and Crown Prince Hirohito's visit, that the two dynasties finally reconnected. In 1971, fifty years after his first visit, Emperor Hirohito returned to the United Kingdom. It was time for Elizabeth II to reciprocate. In the autumn of 1974 it was announced that a six-day state visit would take place the following spring. The British ambassador to Japan at the time, Sir Hugh Cortazzi, was greatly impressed by the Queen's professionalism during what was his first royal tour: 'The impeccable way in which she had been briefed was noted. There were no muffed lines or wrong names. This must have involved many hours of preparation and memorising information.'[28]

In Kyoto, wearing a pillbox hat embellished with pompoms and ostrich feathers, the Queen was initiated into the famous ritual of the tea ceremony. The Duke of Edinburgh, for his part, was particularly intrigued by *kemari*, an ancient sport that resembles football and is played wearing formal court wear. Despite the show of mutual respect, however, relations were not always straightforward. This is demonstrated, for instance, by the many organisational difficulties the embassy came up against, of which the Tokyo procession is an excellent example. As was customary, Buckingham Palace wished to include a tour of the capital in an open car on the agenda, so that the people could see the sovereign. Such an event was inconceivable for the Emperor and his army of chamberlains, however. The imperial family lived behind the palace gates, hidden from view. In front of their emperor, the Japanese people would lower their eyes. What would be the point of such a display? Elizabeth II stood firm, however, and the historic tour was on the brink of being cancelled. The officials therefore came up with a compromise: they would agree to the tour provided that the convoy, which would be made up of cars with tinted windows, drove at a minimum of 60 km/h (37 mph). In London, this was judged absurd. In the end, the Japanese conceded, and on 9 May Queen Elizabeth's procession set out, greeted with cheers by the people of Tokyo.

Kyoto   10 May 1975

TWO HATS FOR THE PRICE OF ONE

I n 1977 the British people were preparing to celebrate Queen Elizabeth II's Silver Jubilee, marking 25 years since her accession to the throne. The general mood was far from celebratory, however. The country was suffering an economic crisis, and in 1976, to prevent it from going under, James Callaghan's government had been forced to request assistance from the International Monetary Fund. With circumstances looking decidedly bleak, the Silver Jubilee was intended to give people a lift.

On the evening of 6 June, carrying a torch in her hand, the Queen started the first of an enormous chain of bonfires designed to light up the whole of the United Kingdom. The next day a million people rushed to London, following in the footsteps of the royal family, who were making their way to St Paul's Cathedral in carriages and landaus for a service of thanksgiving. The Gold State Coach was even called into service for the occasion: the most impressive, and most uncomfortable, of all the state carriages, which has been used for royal coronations since the time of George IV. When she left the cathedral, however, the Queen chose to return to the Guildhall (where luncheon awaited her) on foot, so that she could walk among the crowds.

Beyond the event itself – there would be many more jubilees, after all – one object in particular has entered into history, and even into popular culture: the hat the Queen wore that day. Indeed, it is with this hat that the third series of *The Crown* – produced by Netflix and loosely based on the lives of the Windsors – begins. This was not, however, the first time the Queen had worn this pink beret embellished with bellflowers, designed by Frederick Fox. In a series of audio recordings produced for the British Library in 2003 and 2004, Fox recounts the incredible story behind the headpiece. It was originally made for the royal visit to the United States in July 1976, but the Queen had been unable to wear it because of bad weather. In the end, it made its debut at the Olympic Games in Montreal on 17 July 1976.

At St Paul's Cathedral on 7 June 1977, however, the Queen was supposed to be wearing a different headpiece, indeed a completely different outfit altogether – one designed by Hardy Amies, as Fox recalled: 'We went to the Palace a week before the Jubilee to propose a very pretty light dress made of apple green organza, a coat and matching hat covered with little cream flowers with a touch of green all around.'[29] Elizabeth agreed, proclaiming it the perfect ensemble. But 7 June dawned cold and grey. In front of his television, Fox shivered: 'I thought to myself, there's no way she could wear it; she'll be frozen stiff. I was absolutely delighted, therefore, when I saw she had chosen the bright pink outfit. It was the perfect choice, no doubt about it!'[30]

In 2016, on the Queen's ninetieth birthday, the Royal Collection Trust held an exhibition to celebrate her wardrobe. The emblematic pink bellflower hat occupied a key place in the display. Imagine the curators' surprise, however, when they discovered that there was in the royal archive an identical hat to that made by Fox, designed by the other leading milliner at the time: Simone Mirman. Had Buckingham Palace asked her to make a copy of the original? And if so, why? Which version did the Queen wear for her jubilee? The milliners have taken their secrets with them.

London   7 June 1977

THE LADIES OF THE BAHAMAS

T he Silver Jubilee was also an opportunity for a Commonwealth tour. After visiting the Pacific in the spring, the Queen and Prince Philip travelled to the Caribbean in the autumn. On 19 October the yacht *Britannia* berthed in the Port of Nassau, in the Bahamas. The royals landed in the middle of Junkimoo season, the local carnival, which is filled with traditional dances and generous swigs of rum. Queen Elizabeth chose a green-and-white ensemble with a floral pattern and knotted collar, typical of the 1970s, accompanied by a Breton hat made by Simone Mirman in the same fabric. It was a loose-fitting outfit, ideal for the islands' hot, humid climate. The Queen had to swap it in the middle of the afternoon, however, for an evening dress and tiara, to open Parliament.

Older readers may remember the arrival of other Windsors, the former King Edward VIII and his wife, Wallis, who landed on the island on 17 August 1940. The Duke had just been appointed Governor-General of the Bahamas, in an attempt to keep him away from Berlin and thereby avert some dubious political calculations on his part. In the middle of the Second World War, Edward had decided he had a role to play, and that he could intervene with the Third Reich to secure a peace agreement no one wanted. Lest the Duke find himself kidnapped by the

WHEN SHE LOVES A HAT, IT BECOMES A FRIEND.

Simone Mirman

Nazis, Winston Churchill dispatched him to the other side of the world, appointing him puppet governor of an archipelago with no real strategic importance. In this little corner of paradise, where they wanted for nothing, Edward and Wallis languished in boredom.

With nothing to occupy them, they fled to the United States as soon as the opportunity presented itself.

Whether it was about the Duchess's first facelift or her famous shopping sprees, their trips to New York certainly got people talking. Wallis insisted she was no spendthrift, however, and that she bought only a hundred or so dresses a year. In reality, though, fashion was the only area in which she could reign. Buckingham Palace had been very clear: in the Bahamas, as in London, under no circumstances should the Duchess use the title Her Royal Highness. For a twice-divorced schemer, 'Your Grace' would more than suffice. When the Duke and Duchess left the Bahamas in 1945, no one batted an eyelid.

Elizabeth II and Philip's stay – which lasted just two days – was very modest by comparison. However, with the economic crisis looming large, in a country in which almost 25 per cent of the population were unemployed, the pomp of the royal visit still rubbed some people up the wrong way. According to the Associated Press, the stop came at a cost of 250,000 dollars. The Queen and the Duke of Edinburgh bid farewell to their hosts on 20 October to set sail for the Virgin Islands, Antigua and Barbados, where other parliaments awaited them.

Meanwhile, thousands of kilometres away, their son Charles was making headlines for his romantic dalliances, real and imagined. After Tricia, the daughter of President Nixon, and Princess Marie-Astrid of Luxembourg – both of whom had attended his investiture in 1969 – the heir to the throne was rumoured to be in a relationship with Lady Sarah Spencer, Diana's older sister. The liaison did not last long, however. The people of Britain and the Bahamas would have to wait a while longer before the Queen's eldest son found himself a spouse, who would later become Queen Consort of the Bahamas.

Nassau   19 October 1977

A HIGH-RISK MISSION

'We are faced with a very difficult decision.' Addressing the House of Commons, Prime Minister Margaret Thatcher could not mask her unease. Could her government allow the Queen to travel to Zambia, on the last leg of a tour of southern Africa that was due to commence in a few days' time? The problem was the civil war that had been ravaging Southern Rhodesia (now Zimbabwe) since the 1960s, since Zimbabwe bordered Zambia, where the guerrillas had established their rear base. Led by Joshua Nkomo, a friend of Robert Mugabe, there were nearly 20,000 rebels on Zambian territory. Equipped with Soviet anti-aircraft missiles, they had even managed to bring down two airliners. It was enough to send shivers down the spines of Buckingham Palace and Downing Street. Yet the Queen stood firm: she was resolved to open the Commonwealth conference scheduled to take place at the start of August in Lusaka, the capital of Zambia. Her credibility – and the future of the organisation – depended on it.

In this electric ambiance, the royal family's chartered jet – the Queen was travelling with Prince Philip and their son Prince Andrew – landed on Zambian soil on 27 July 1979, having carefully avoided the airspace of Southern Rhodesia. Dressed all in yellow and sporting a felt cloche hat decorated with

huge flowers, Elizabeth greeted President Kenneth Kaunda, who had come to welcome her in person. Kaunda introduced her to the dignitaries of the regime, who were standing in line on the tarmac. Nkomo had also been invited to attend, but, furious at being depicted as a terrorist by the British press, he chose not to make an appearance. He did nonetheless keep his promise of a ceasefire.

The banners that were brandished as the Queen passed by were not all in her honour, however. On some of them, support for the rebellion was spelled out in black and white: 'Welcome to Zambia, the border between democracy, peace and freedom, and apartheid, oppression and slavery.' Another declared: 'Don't sell out Zimbabwe in your speech to Commonwealth.' By opening the conference on 1 August, however, the Queen demonstrated that she would not be intimidated, and above all that dialogue between the Member States must be maintained at all costs: 'While the political landscape tossed and turned around her, the Queen worked away calmly behind the scenes … mediating between enemy factions, offering advice, making suggestions, and encouraging positive initiatives.'[31] The Zambians took note. On the day of her departure, a choir sang: 'Bye, bye, Queenie, come again.' Michael Shea, the royal press secretary, rejoiced: 'The tour was a sensation; the best yet.'[32] Elizabeth returned to Great Britain crowned with success, and was able to set off for a very well-earned holiday at Balmoral, as she did every summer. The break was to be short-lived, however; on 27 August 1979 the IRA blew up Lord Mountbatten's fishing boat. Uncle Dickie died on the spot, and three others were injured.

Lusaka   27 July 1979

A NIGHT-MARE IN THE SUNSHINE

I n 1980 Elizabeth II went on a tour of the Mediterranean. After visiting Italy and the Vatican, she travelled on to the Maghreb: first Tunisia, then Algeria and, lastly, Morocco, where she was expected for her first state visit. It was a historic moment that quickly turned into a nightmare for her and her entourage, leading the journalist and filmmaker Robert Hardman to describe it as 'the most chaotic visit of her reign'.[33] The problem was the suspicious, completely unpredictable character of King Hassan II, who had been on the throne since 1961. The king would disrupt the official programme as he saw fit, disappearing without warning, and even seeming resistant to the very notion of being on time – while Elizabeth herself was punctuality personified.

On the first evening, in a taste of what was to come, the Queen had to wait in her car for an hour because the banquet organised in her honour was not ready on time. The following day, her nerves began to be truly put to the test. At a luncheon organised in her honour in the desert, the Queen's host gave her the slip. Time dragged on in the tent put up for the British delegation. As the hours ticked by, they watched a series of traditional dances and equestrian displays. The King of Morocco was nowhere to be seen. The photographs betray the troubles of

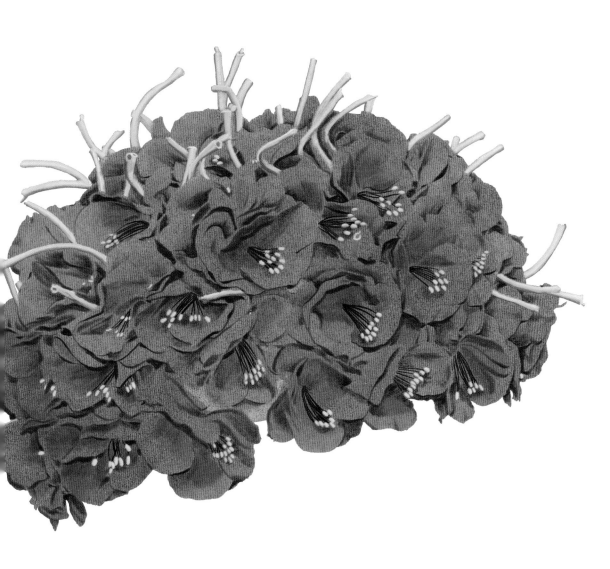

the day by immortalising a somewhat vexed – and hungry – Queen, wearing a hat made of silk poppies created by Simone Mirman. By the time King Hassan finally reappeared – for what was supposed to be a luncheon – it was four o'clock in the afternoon. The Brits were invited to take their places at the table. Hassan ate with his fingers, as was customary. Did he think this would faze Elizabeth? The Queen, who, according to her entourage, had managed wonderfully when presented with a plate of grilled lamb but no cutlery a few days earlier in Algeria, refused the knife and fork offered to her.

Royal patience nonetheless has its limits. 'Kindly refrain from addressing my members of staff in that manner,' she snapped at Hassan, who was ranting and raving at one of her private secretaries. She was equally firm when the king wished to stop the convoy in order to get out of a visit that she held particularly dear. 'Very well,' she declared. 'Stop the car in that case. I will take my own escort.'

On the last evening of the eventful trip, it was Elizabeth's turn to invite the King of Morocco to one final reception, on board *Britannia*. True to form, Hassan let it be known that he would not be on time, and requested that the start of the festivities be delayed. 'Impossible', responded the Queen, reassuring him that his lateness would be forgiven. Furious, the king arrived at the royal yacht with a far larger retinue than anticipated. For a moment, it looked as though there would not be enough seats to go around. Elizabeth rode out the storm, however, displaying the utmost tact. The following day Hassan declared himself enchanted by the visit. So enchanted, in fact, that he went to London on a state visit in 1987, at Her Majesty's invitation.

Marrakech   27 October 1980

THE WEDDING OF THE CENTURY

O n 29 July 1981 some 750 million television viewers watched the wedding of the Prince of Wales and the young Lady Diana Spencer. Extravagance was the order of the day. Forsaking Westminster Abbey, the bride and groom chose instead to exchange their vows at St Paul's Cathedral. This was the first time a royal wedding had been held at the cathedral since 1501, when it had witnessed the marriage of Prince Arthur, Henry VII's eldest son, and Catherine of Aragon. Diana's now iconic dress was an explosion of ivory taffeta, featuring a train 8 m (26 ft) long that only just fitted into the coach transporting her to St Paul's. (Rumour has it the bride wanted an even longer train.) The dress was designed by David and Elizabeth Emanuel, two young designers recently out of college, selected by Diana herself. 'We played up the theatrical side. It was the image everyone had of a fairy-tale princess. It was the right time for it. Frills and flounces were all the rage,' the designers told the BBC. The wedding of the century did not bring them much luck, however. In spite of the global publicity – or perhaps because of it – their fashion house went under and the couple ended up getting divorced.

In the face of this media storm – and it was merely the beginning – the Queen did not change one iota. The indispensable Norman Hartnell, who passed away

SHE LIKES VERY SIMPLE THINGS. SHE DOES NOT GO IN FOR ANYTHING QUIRKY.

Simone Mirman

in 1979, was succeeded by his disciple the dressmaker Ian Thomas, who designed and made her dress in silk crêpe de Chine. Hartnell had entrusted Simone Mirman with making the Queen's hat for Princess Anne's wedding in 1973, and Thomas did the same for Charles's in 1981. The two hats were in fact very similar, although the first was more like a headscarf – a specialist area for the milliner in the 1970s – while the second was closer in style to a beret, adorned with tiny satin flowers. Mirman loved both styles of headdress for the Queen. 'They suit her so well,' she told a journalist a few months later. 'I want to create something new for the Queen, to move away from the flowers and feathers we have seen her in over the past ten years.'[34]

Mirman did not make the Princess of Wales's hats, however. Was this a source of regret for the milliner? 'She needs to craft her own style, choose her own milliners, support the next generation. It's all part of her role.'[35] With the young, beautiful, popular Diana, milliners started to hope that hats would enjoy a return to favour. Whatever Diana wore, people snapped it up. For about £100, you could get your hands on one of the Princess of Wales's fascinators. Diana even managed the incredible feat of bringing the 1940s veil back into fashion. The young woman was still finding her feet, though. Philip Somerville helped to point her in the right direction. While before she had always worn small hats, the milliner convinced her to try huge wide-brimmed headpieces, creating the 'Flying Saucer' model – worn on the side of the head – especially for her. The style was a real revolution and an act of self-affirmation; even the Queen was won over by these novel 'saucers'.

London   29 July 1981

WHO TRIED TO KILL THE QUEEN?

'The Queen and Prince Philip will be very sad to leave New Zealand today, after what has been one of their most successful and enjoyable visits. As the Queen said in her speech yesterday, they have been very moved by the incredible welcome they have received in New Zealand and feel perfectly at home here.'[36] As soon as they left Auckland, their officials were flooded with words of thanks. In spite of the crisis in Northern Ireland and the repercussions it was having at the international level, the Queen's sixth visit – she visited ten times between 1953 and 2002 – went flawlessly. Between May and August 1981, ten young Irish prisoners starved themselves to death in a protest against their English 'occupier'. When Elizabeth II and the Duke of Edinburgh made their first stop in Australia, there were real fears of disorder. Eamon O'Connor, an Irishman living in Sydney, had also gone on hunger strike. His state of health was a cause for concern. If he died while the Queen and her husband were in Australia, would it further aggravate the situation? Operation 'Fortress' was triggered.

In New Zealand, others sympathetic to the Irish cause were preparing to demonstrate their anti-Windsor sentiments. The royal 'walkabouts' were still scheduled to go ahead, however. In Wellington, a tour was even organised for the royals in a Land Rover

116
—
117

convertible, so that they could get out and meet the public once again. Wearing a pink felt hat made by Marie O'Regan – the favourite milliner of dressmaker Ian Thomas – the Queen was regaled with dozens of bouquets of flowers. Children were even permitted to follow the car. Only 15 or so opponents tried to disrupt the visit, shouting 'Ireland free, get troops out!' Things could well have been worse.

On 14 October 1981, however, while the couple were dining with Prime Minister Robert Muldoon at his home, they heard an explosion, the origin of which could not be identified. The press reported this quasi-news item, along with a false alarm from the same morning in Dunedin, a town in the south: 'A shot was fired while the Queen was travelling across town by car. The police have since arrested a man who was shooting birds on his own land.'[37] It was not until 2018 and the declassification of sensitive information that the mysterious hunter was identified as an unbalanced 17-year-old called Christopher John Lewis, who was trying to kill not birds but rather the Queen. 'It may be the closest anyone has ever come to assassinating Queen Elizabeth II,' reported *The Guardian*.[38] Armed with a shotgun, the young man fired at the Queen as she was getting out of her car. No one was injured, but the event was sufficiently embarrassing to be covered up. The gunman remained a source of concern for the authorities for several years, such that when the Queen returned to Australia in 1995, they paid for him to go away on holiday so as to keep him at a distance.

Wellington   14 October 1981

THE QUEEN ON THE OTHER SIDE OF THE WORLD

T hirty years after her accession to the throne, Elizabeth II visited Tuvalu – her smallest kingdom, with a population of less than 8,000 – for the very first time. Having gained independence in 1978, the archipelago elected to keep Elizabeth II as its head of state. There, she was not the Queen of the United Kingdom, however, but rather, according to the Tuvaluan Constitution, 'Queen of Tuvalu, by the grace of God'. She arrived on shore in the manner of a Polynesian queen, aboard a traditional dugout canoe decorated with palm leaves and painted in the national colours, turquoise and gold. On the beach, Tuvaluans hoisted the boats on to their shoulders and carried the Queen and the Duke of Edinburgh through the streets of Funafuti, the capital, singing. In his speech, Prime Minister Tomasi Puapua thanked the Prince Consort for keeping the promise he had made during his first visit, in 1959: to return one day with his wife: 'Tuvalu may well be poor in terms of surface area and natural resources, but we believe, Your Majesty, that happiness, culture and conviviality are more important than material riches.'[39]

Tuvalu did not take long to cast its unique spell. Among the royal entourage, word quickly got around that the Queen had never enjoyed herself so much. 'Contrary to the somewhat reserved, dignified image

120
—
121

she gives off, she has taken the most unusual situations as they come and, in characteristically good spirits, she has enjoyed every moment,' related Grania Forbes, the British Press Association correspondent reporting on the royal tour.

The day after her arrival, the Queen wore a turquoise dress, in what appeared to be a nod to the flag of the archipelago. Since her pillbox hat, which was decorated with a huge rose, was not enough to protect her from the blazing sunshine, she also carried a parasol while visiting the island's main institutions: the Princess-Margaret Hospital – opened by her sister three years earlier – and the post office. As testament to the historic nature of the visit, the Queen was presented with three new postage stamps designed in her honour. The sovereign was also invited to lay the first stone of the new Parliament, a task for which she put on a pair of gloves.

Last of all, in what was no doubt the highlight of the tour, the Queen was taken to see the palm tree that her son Prince Charles had planted 12 years previously. She was the last member of her family to visit Tuvalu. Alas, all good things must come to an end, and Elizabeth and Philip returned to *Britannia* to continue their voyage. They were once again transported in canoes carried through the streets by men. Inclement weather played its part on this occasion, however. Two young girls, each carrying an umbrella, were charged with protecting the royal couple from the rain. Yet the closer they came to the beach, the worse the storm became. While the Polynesian crew rowed towards the royal yacht, torrential rain poured down on Tuvalu. The Queen and Prince Philip were soaked, yet in excellent spirits.

CHARMING COMPANY

A t last, a sunny spell. The day after she arrived in Jordan, the Queen finally took out her sunglasses and tried to relax. King Hussein took her to visit some of the royal stables, a programme that would normally have delighted her, had it not been for the overbearing presence of the security forces and the grave tensions gripping the Middle East. As the King of Jordan's thoroughbreds paraded in front of them, Elizabeth and Philip asked their hosts about the tank gunfire that could be heard reverberating through the Jordan Valley, just a few kilometres away. They were told it was a training operation. Two days earlier, a bomb had gone off in Amman. The Jordanian Army was on high alert, as was Jim Beaton, the detective responsible for the Queen's security, who did not let her out of his sight for one second. Beaton had already distinguished himself for his bravery during the attempted kidnap of Princess Anne ten years earlier.

Throughout the trip, the Queen and Prince Philip hardly saw any Jordanians. 'It was more like a private visit than a state one. Because of the paranoiac levels of security throughout the trip, there were hardly any crowds,' reported the *Sunday Mirror* on 1 April. On 29 March drastic measures were taken at the site of Petra: residents living nearby were kept at a strict

distance and a military helicopter flew over the site non-stop for more than four hours.

In this challenging context, the Queen was attacked … for her style! The green anise pillbox hat decorated with flower stamens and small blooms, made for her by the milliner Valerie Lee, was not a hit, nor were the ensembles designed by her dressmaker Ian Thomas. The Queen's hats were no longer all the rage, any more than her audacious colour choices: candy pink, turquoise and emerald green. 'There have been a couple of unpleasant comments about the Queen's outfits, with the sovereign being described as frumpy in Jordan. According to her critics, her clothing choices are doing nothing to boost fashion,' reported a tabloid newspaper mockingly, lamenting what it described as 'another royal racket' for her image.[40]

The criticism was rendered even more unkind by the comparisons made throughout the trip between Elizabeth and her influential counterpart Queen Noor, who had just turned 33 and stood over 1.8 m (6 ft) tall in high heels: 'While the Queen often seemed sombre and troubled, her host's wife, Queen Noor, was positively beaming.'[41] Whether she was sporting a Mondrian suit by Yves Saint Laurent on the airport tarmac or a turban in the Bedouins' tent, photographers had found a new idol in this young American woman of Syrian, Lebanese and Swedish origin, catapulted into the world of royalty in 1978 after a fairy-tale wedding – King Hussein's fourth. The Queen of Jordan was 'ready to take on the role of Queen of Glamour left vacant by the passing of Princess Grace' of Monaco, enthused an editorial writer, noting in passing that Prince Philip was 'charmed by this pretty young thing'.[42]

Amman   27 March 1984

MADE FOR CHINA

E lizabeth II was on good form. She was practically running. After landing on 12 October in Beijing, where Prince Philip awaited her, she barely drew breath before throwing herself wholeheartedly into a historic six-day tour of China. The festivities began the following day, in Tiananmen Square, where the Queen and her husband were greeted by 21 cannon shots. Sporting a red coat and a plaited straw hat and surrounded by the fluttering flags of the People's Republic, Elizabeth blended right in.

'The Chinese people have been waiting for Her Majesty and the Duke of Edinburgh to visit China for a long time. Today, this wish has become a reality,' muttered President Li Xiannian, who was visibly delighted despite his eyes being hidden behind dark glasses.[43] In reality, though, the Chinese people barely knew who the Queen was in 1986; some even mistook her for Margaret Thatcher, who had visited two years earlier. 'I very much look forward to Princess Margaret's visit next year and I would be delighted if Prince Charles and Princess Diana were to visit too,' said President Li.[44] The message got through: Margaret and her children visited in May 1987, while the Prince and Princess of Wales settled for a visit to Hong Kong in 1989.

When they were not engaged in discussions with senior Communist Party officials, Elizabeth and Philip treated themselves to a few tourist outings, providing yet another opportunity for the Duke of Edinburgh to distinguish himself through his embarrassing quips. Essential sights included the Terracotta Army of Xi'an – discovered in 1974 – and, of course, the Great Wall. To visit the latter, on 14 October the couple were taken to the site of Badaling, 80 km (50 miles) from Beijing. An excellent walker accustomed to long hikes in the Scottish Highlands, the Queen strode across the structure for more than 40 minutes. 'The descent will be worse than the ascent,[45] she said to the breathless members of her delegation.

The Queen's suit – designed by Kenneth Fleetwood, Hardy Amies' assistant and later his artistic director – was not the most practical of choices. But after the red chosen for Tiananmen Square, the imperial purple flattered the Chinese people and delighted observers all over the world. Her hat – made to match by Frederick Fox – had the same effect. The milliner did not have much time to reflect on it, however. Only alerted by Margaret MacDonald, the Queen's dresser, at the very last minute – 'Mr Fox, something terrible has happened: I've made a mistake!' – Fox had had to work in haste, essentially blindly: 'Occasionally I had to make pieces for the Queen without seeing her outfit, out of the blue really, when someone had forgotten to make a hat. So, I had to make the hat and deliver it even though I only found out at lunchtime [and] despite her being due to leave the next morning! These things happened, in the royal family too.'[46]

Badaling   14 October 1986

THE TALKING HAT

'I hope you can see me today.' The Queen's sense of humour was right on the mark. Gathered for Congress, the senators and members of the House of Representatives burst out laughing. Her disastrous appearance two days earlier on the White House lawn was still at the front of everyone's minds. Having arrived in Washington on 14 May 1991, just three months after the end of the Gulf War, the Queen was invited to deliver her first address. She extended a few words of thanks to George H.W. Bush, from whom she took the stand: a simple formality. The problem was that the American President was tall – 6ft 2in – while the Queen, at just 5ft 3in, was much more petite. No one had thought to sneak a step on to the stage between the two addresses, however. Elizabeth therefore found herself confronted with a lectern that was far too high for her. Throughout her speech, all the journalists could see was her straw hat, made by Frederick Fox. A talking hat! The quip made headlines around the world. After this mishap, her speech at Congress the following day needed to be perfect. A platform, hidden from the spectators, had already been set up.

While Congress was accustomed to royal visits – eight sovereigns had taken the floor before the Queen – the wearing of hats had been prohibited

since 1837. Back then, the fashion for top hats did to some extent interfere with the debates, so the Americans ruled that their elected representatives should sit bareheaded. Faced with the same problem, however, the English chose not to be able to see, only too happy to use the hat as a symbol of independence from the monarchy – since one had to remove one's hat in the presence of the king. For the visit in 1991, Buckingham Palace requested that an exception be made to the rule and that the Queen be exempted from the requirement to remove her hat. Donnald K. Anderson, Clerk of the House, was delighted to be able to satisfy the Palace's wishes at such little cost. He quickly agreed, justifying the decision to his colleagues by barking: 'The Queen is the Queen.' This great honour had in fact already been granted to Queen Juliana of the Netherlands in 1952, as well as to her daughter Queen Beatrix in 1982, both of whom appeared in Congress wearing hats.

The Queen received hearty applause after her 15-minute address, as well as a standing ovation for her 'God bless America'. Some elected representatives chose to boycott the occasion, however, including Joseph Kennedy II, the representative from Massachusetts (and nephew of the deceased President John F. Kennedy), who deplored the violence underway in Northern Ireland; and Gus Savage, the representative from Illinois, who opposed the lifting of the British embargo on South Africa, which had still not abolished apartheid.

This trip to the United States also provided the Queen with an opportunity to get to know the Bush clan better, especially George W. Bush, whom at the time no one expected to become President. The journalist Robert Hardman has recounted a funny anecdote in his regard. After he had been introduced to her as a free spirit, the Queen asked George W. if he was the black sheep of the family. He agreed, to which the Queen replied, reassuringly: 'Every family has one.'[47]

Washington   14 May 1991

ANNUS HORRIBILIS

'[This] is not a year on which I shall look back with undiluted pleasure.' On 24 November 1992 Elizabeth II addressed the 500 guests gathered at the Guildhall in London for a luncheon to mark the fortieth anniversary of her accession to the throne. The atmosphere was decidedly gloomy. The dark green velvet chosen by Frederick Fox – the Queen wore a Breton hat trimmed with silk – was so sombre that she looked as though she was in mourning. Four days earlier, a fire had ravaged Windsor Castle for 15 hours. The following day Elizabeth had visited the site to check the extent of the damage, which was estimated to be in the region of £60 million.

As awful as it had been, however, the fire was far from the Queen's only concern. This had been a year of unparalleled scandal for the Windsors, leaving a lasting mark on the image of the monarchy. In January, compromising photographs were published in *Paris Match*, showing the Duchess of York in the company of a Texan millionaire. Sarah Ferguson and Prince Andrew separated on 19 March. Just over a month later, on 23 April, Princess Anne and Mark Phillips' divorce was at last finalised; their marriage had been plagued by rumour and disclosures for years. In the summer, just as Andrew and Sarah seemed to be sorting things out, new photographs hit the tabloids:

138
—
139

in one of them, the provocative duchess's toe was being sucked by her financial adviser. Unfortunately for her, Sarah Ferguson was at Balmoral with the royal family when this latest bomb went off. She was asked to cut her trip short and leave the premises.

The biggest scandal, however, undoubtedly concerned the star couple: Charles and Diana. On 7 June the journalist Andrew Morton released his explosive biography, *Diana, Her True Story*. Stupefied, the British people learned that the Princess had attempted to take her own life, that she was bulimic, and that Charles had by no means cut ties with his ex-girlfriend Camilla Parker Bowles. The copies flew off the shelves. 'It was utter chaos; the biggest catastrophe to strike the royal family since the abdication,' Morton recalled.[48] The worst was yet to come, however. In November, the first extracts of a telephone conversation between Charles and Camilla were leaked, recorded without their knowledge in 1989. The tabloids had a field day with the story, nicknamed 'Camillagate', and the full transcript was published in January 1993.

'There can be no doubt, of course, that criticism is good for people and institutions that are part of public life,' the Queen acknowledged with a resigned air during her speech at the Guildhall. 'I sometimes wonder how future generations will judge the events of this tumultuous year. I dare say that history will take a slightly more moderate view than that of some contemporary commentators. Distance is well known to lend enchantment, even to the less attractive views. After all, it has the inestimable advantage of hindsight.'

London   24 November 1992

THE MAGNUM OPUS

'We now have a common land border, Madam,' declared François Mitterrand, hitting the nail on the head. The creation of the Channel Tunnel had brought the United Kingdom and France a little closer. Bringing a dream dating back two centuries to reality, 4,000 French workers and 7,000 British ones had come together to achieve an astounding feat of technical prowess. The American Society of Civil Engineers immediately hailed the construction as one of the Seven Wonders of the Modern World, alongside the Empire State Building, the Panama Canal and the Golden Gate Bridge. Its inauguration by the two heads of state was a historic moment, involving a meticulous programme scripted down to the tiniest details. At 9.52 a.m. the first Eurostar from London left Waterloo station. A hero for the day, the driver Nigel Brown was responsible for this inaugural journey and the 650 passengers on board. Among them were two people close to his heart: the Queen and his own mother, Anne Brown.

The train reached the entrance to the tunnel at Folkestone a few minutes late, after being forced to slow down so that it did not arrive before the French delegation, who had boarded at Lille-Europe station. The two Eurostars met on the French side, in Coquelles. Under a light drizzle, Queen Elizabeth

142
—
143

met Mitterrand, no doubt the French president for whom she had the greatest fondness. For the occasion, she wore a pillbox hat by Marie O'Regan in fuchsia velvet, decorated with an enormous bow. The milliner herself declared the piece to be as much a sculpture as a hat: 'Hat-making is very similar to the work of a sculptor. When I was young, I would have loved to go to art school and make it my trade,' she confessed 27 years later.[49] Her 'sculpted' pillbox hats earned her great renown, and her polka-dot model, worn by the Queen in Hungary in 1993 and created using the same techniques, has also gone down in history.[50]

On 6 May 1994 at 1 p.m., the Queen and the French President cut the symbolic three-coloured ribbon of Calais lace. Then came the speeches, delivered in French by both parties. 'This is the first time in history that the heads of state of France and Great Britain have met without having to take a boat or plane,' Elizabeth declared. Mitterrand himself was yet to cross the English Channel. He was invited to get into the Queen's Rolls-Royce, which was loaded into one of the wagons. President and sovereign travelled to Folkestone sitting next to each other on the rear seat. 'An English vehicle', declared the British newspapers the following day, with amusement; despite the shuttle, they had lost none of the superiority complex typical of island nations. One journalist nonetheless felt the need to specify that 'Great Britain may have supplied the Rolls-Royce for the inaugural journey, but France supplied the lunch: a sumptuous menu consisting of sole and duck.'[51]

THE WORLD MOURNS DIANA

London
5 September 1997

T he royal family were still at Balmoral. Four days after the death of Diana, while the country mourned 'the people's princess', the silence of the Windsors themselves was deafening. Worse still, they seemed to have no intention of returning to London. 'Where is our Queen?' asked *The Sun*, while *The Mirror* appealed to her directly: 'Your people are suffering; talk to us, Your Majesty.' By choosing not to react, the royal family left itself open to the most vehement criticism. They were accused of a lack of feeling, of disdain, and worse. Faced with this avalanche of reproaches, on 4 September Buckingham Palace finally issued a statement: 'The Royal Family have been hurt by suggestions that they are indifferent to the country's sorrow at the tragic death of the Princess of Wales. The princess was a much-loved national figure, but she was also a mother whose sons miss her deeply. Prince William and Prince Harry themselves want to be with their father and their grandparents at this time in the quiet haven of Balmoral.' The statement failed to convince, and the gulf between the Queen and her subjects seemed unbridgeable.

On 5 September, the day before the funeral, the Queen and her loved ones finally made their way back to London. Elizabeth and the Duke of Edinburgh at last set eyes on the mountains of flowers that had piled

148
—
149

up in front of the gates of Buckingham Palace. The Queen was dressed in mourning: a suit and a black velvet Breton hat made by Frederick Fox. Prince Philip carefully laid down the bouquets handed to him in tribute to Diana. The sovereign, for her part, took the time to exchange a few words with the crowd, supposedly so hostile towards her. One man from Wandsworth in south London recalled: 'The Queen passed in front of me; she seemed very sad. I said: "Welcome home, Your Majesty." She looked me right in the eye and nodded.'[52] A woman who had travelled all the way from Glasgow whispered to her: 'You must be very brave to have come to see us today.'[53] The occasion left such an impression that it provided the inspiration behind one of the most mythical scenes of Stephen Frears' film *The Queen* nine years later.

When Elizabeth and Philip took their leave, the crowd began clapping. Fifteen minutes later, the couple set off for St James's Palace, where the Princess of Wales's remains lay in state. After signing the book of condolence, the Queen once again went out to meet the people, in all their grief. She was again applauded; clearly all was not lost. That same evening, at 6 p.m., she addressed the nation on live television from the Chinese drawing room of her London residence, wearing glasses but no hat. Through the open window behind her, viewers could see the thousands of people who continued to gather, carrying flowers. 'Since last Sunday's dreadful news we have seen, throughout Britain and around the world, an overwhelming expression of sadness at Diana's death. We have all been trying in our different ways to cope. It is not easy to express a sense of loss, since the initial shock is often succeeded by a mixture of other feelings: disbelief, incomprehension, anger – and concern for those who remain. We have all felt those emotions in these last few days.'

END OF AN ERA

T he royal family gathered in full for a final farewell to *Britannia*, which was being decommissioned after 44 years of service. The on-board clocks had all been stopped at exactly 3.01 p.m., the time at which the Queen last disembarked from the ship. Elizabeth wiped away a tear. She was wearing a hat by Marie O'Regan: a toque made of moulded fabric folded like a turban. It was a truly sculptural piece, and one the milliner still remembered at the age of 96: 'For that hat, I had to come up with a style, which I presented to the Queen. Then we had to choose the felt. When we couldn't find the right shade, though, we decided to make it in the fabric from her coat.'

The *Britannia* deserved nothing less. The boat, the eighty-third royal ship, was a haven for the family, away from the worries and events of the world. The Queen travelled the seas of the globe on it. The apartments on board consisted of a bedroom, an antechamber, a study, a sitting room and a bathroom. The Duke of Edinburgh even had his own smoking room, where he could welcome officers. The crew washed down the deck every day before 8 a.m. in complete silence; they communicated using sign language so as not to disturb the passengers. The sailors had to be impeccably dressed at all times, even in the tropics; if they wished to grow a beard, they

152
—
153

TO ME, THEY ARE NOT JUST HATS; THEY ARE WORKS OF ART.

Marie O'Regan

had to request permission six months in advance and learn to trim it themselves so that they never appeared unkempt in front of the sovereign. The royal yacht covered more than 2 million km (1.2 million miles). A veritable tool of British diplomacy, it enabled the Queen, who reigned over no fewer than 16 countries, to go out and meet her people and uphold the ties of the Commonwealth. Members of the royal family had even set off on their honeymoons on board *Britannia*: Princess Margaret and Antony Armstrong-Jones; Princess Anne and Mark Phillips; Prince Charles and Lady Diana Spencer; Prince Andrew and Sarah Ferguson … Four marriages, and four divorces!

In 1997 Tony Blair's government decided it was time to decommission the ageing vessel. Since then, it has enjoyed a peaceful retirement in the port of Leith, near Edinburgh. Now a museum, *Britannia* attracts more than 250,000 tourists a year, all eager to discover her pontoon and the private lives of the royal family. A few nostalgic souls dream of a new royal yacht. Sir Donald Gosling, a wealthy entrepreneur, even bequeathed £50 million to the royal family to build a second *Britannia*: a pharaonic, somewhat fanciful project supported at one point by Boris Johnson, before he became prime minister. There is a good chance that *Britannia* will never have a successor, however. In July 2011 she welcomed the royal family one last time for a reception to celebrate the marriage of Zara Phillips, Princess Anne's daughter, to the rugby player Mike Tindall.

Portsmouth   11 December 1997

HAZARDS OF THE JOB

Kuala Lumpur
21 September 1998

O fficial trips are rarely a walk in the park. However well versed the staff at Buckingham Palace are in the exercise, and however impeccable the logistics, surprises can always arise. The slightest glitch can derail the entire exercise at any time. This is no doubt what Angela Kelly, the Queen's dresser, was afraid of in Malaysia in September 1998. That year, Elizabeth II travelled to Kuala Lumpur to open the Commonwealth Games. For the occasion, Kelly had selected a coral dress and matching hat. Were the preparations behind schedule? Whatever the reason, the fact remains that the Queen took off without having tried on her hat, and Kelly herself had not even seen it. 'Sketches of the hat had been made, but because of Her Majesty's packed schedule, the hat was only delivered at the very last minute,' she recalls.[54]

When she removed it from its wrapping, however, Kelly's heart sank; she could see that the headpiece would not suit the Queen. Visibly displeased, she conveyed her concerns to the sovereign herself, who replied: 'It's a bit late now. What can I wear instead? I'll have to wear it.' Undeterred, the dresser proposed a clever sleight of hand. Since the back of the hat was prettier than the front, the Queen could simply wear it back to front. Time was running out. The sovereign seemed unconvinced.

156
—
157

I AM NEVER COMPLETELY SATISFIED WITH A HAT; IT COULD ALWAYS BE IMPROVED.

Marie O'Regan

She voiced one last concern: what if the milliner who had made the hat was offended? Kelly recalls: 'I told her not to worry and that I would come up with an explanation when we got back to London.'

The ill-fated hat was one of Marie O'Regan's creations. Was she satisfied with the explanation? At the age of 96, she could still not hide her emotions when discussing the incident. Did the experience affect her collaboration with the Palace? The milliner continued to work for the Queen, and at the end of her career in 2005 she even received a royal warrant, establishing her as an official supplier to Her Majesty. Milliners are quickly forgotten once they have left, however. The old lady was not even invited to the major retrospective exhibition organised by Buckingham Palace in 2016 – 'Fashioning a Reign: 90 Years of Style from the Queen's Wardrobe' – despite hundreds of her creations being included. She had to buy her own ticket, just like everyone else.

Kelly, on the other hand, continued her incredible rise to stardom. In the space of 20 years, she went from being completely unknown to the general public – she was of modest origins and born in Liverpool – to shaking up the sector and earning a place for herself at Buckingham Palace. She went on to become Personal Assistant, Adviser and Curator of Jewellery to Her Majesty Queen Elizabeth II, overseeing a totally new wardrobe in which hats still occupied a key place. The pinnacle of her career came on 20 February 2018, when she attended a show at London Fashion Week alongside the Queen and *Vogue* editor-in-chief Anna Wintour, with photographers snapping away. Elizabeth II took the opportunity to award a brand-new prize: the Queen Elizabeth II Award for British Design. The award was a trophy shaped like a rose, designed by Kelly herself.

Kuala Lumpur   21 September 1998

GREETINGS FROM NORWAY

T he royal families of Norway and the United Kingdom have maintained close ties since the early 20th century. In 1905, after five centuries of Danish and then Swedish rule, Norway gained its independence. Having rid themselves of the Bernadotte Dynasty, the Norwegian people elected Prince Carl of Denmark as their new king. The Prince became King Haakon VII, much to the despair of his wife, Princess Maud of the United Kingdom (King George V's sister), who found herself forced to move to Oslo. As soon as the opportunity presented itself, the new Queen of Norway returned to England and to her residence, Appleton House, on the Sandringham estate in Norfolk, where her only son, Alexander – renamed Olav at the age of two – was born. The connection between the two royal families has never been broken.

Queen Elizabeth had a particular fondness for her Norwegian cousins, never missing a chance to see them when they were in London. She made two state visits to Norway, in 1955 and 1981, before agreeing to a third in the spring of 2001. On 30 May 2001 she and Philip were visibly delighted when they were reunited with King Harald V – sixtieth in line to the British throne – and Queen Sonja, who had come to welcome them on the tarmac of Oslo Airport. For the occasion, Elizabeth's

milliner Frederick Fox surpassed himself by revisiting the form of the cloche hat. The headpiece is not dissimilar to the milliner's early creations and the hats he designed in 1968 for Stanley Kubrick's film *2001: A Space Odyssey*.

The visit also provided the Queen and the Duke of Edinburgh with the chance to meet Mette-Marit Tjessem Høiby, Crown Prince Haakon's fiancée and already the mother of a little boy from a previous relationship. As open-minded as the Norwegians were – Queen Sonja was the first commoner to marry a future king – Mette-Marit's past still ruffled some feathers. Having witnessed three of her four children get divorced, Elizabeth looked kindly upon what was clearly a marriage of love. The wedding was due to take place in August.

Elizabeth's own mother, the Queen Mother, herself almost succumbed to Scandinavia's charms at one point. In 1954 Crown Prince Olav lost his wife, Märtha. A widower at the age of 51, he grew close to the Queen Mother, who had lost her husband, George VI, in 1952. She frequently invited Olav to Clarence House, her London residence, and to Royal Lodge, her home on the Windsor estate. It is unlikely that she ever seriously considered marrying the man who would become king of Norway in 1957, but they remained good friends.

A year after the state visit in 2001, Fox retired, marking the end of 35 years of loyal service during which he had made more than 350 hats for the Queen. While interviewing him at his studio, the journalist Yvette Jelfs – herself a milliner – recognised, among the plethora of models on display, the curious hat the sovereign had worn upon her arrival in Oslo. Scrunching up his eyes, Fox declared: 'They copied that one straightaway.' It may have been copied, but it was certainly never equalled.

THE FUTURE IS IN SAFE HANDS

For her Grenadier Guards, the Queen brought out the butterflies. Her dress was dotted with them, as was her hat. Dillon Wallwork, Philip Somerville's assistant and later his artistic director, designed them in fabric, dyed green and studded with gems, with feathers cut to look like antennae. They flutter around the skullcap, on to which the milliner pinned a diamond brooch representing a flaming grenade, the emblem of the regiment, which the Guards wear on the collar of their uniforms. It is a true piece of artistry. With such a hat, the Queen was suitably attired to celebrate the 350th anniversary of one of the five infantry regiments that make up her foot guards (the others are the Coldstream Guards, the Scots Guards, the Irish Guards and the Welsh Guards). The Queen herself was Colonel-in-Chief of all five regiments.

While the Changing of the Guard is an unmissable sight for tourists, those who take part in it are in fact elite troops deployed to serve in the most sensitive operations. The Grenadier Guards, who earned their renown – and their bearskin hats – by crushing the French at Waterloo, have also fought in the Crimean War, the two world wars and, more recently, Afghanistan. Established in 1915, the Welsh Guards experienced life in the trenches, as well as being deployed on

164
—
165

peacekeeping missions in Bosnia. The Scots Guards played a key role in the Falklands War in 1982 and were also deployed in Iraq between 2004 and 2008. Lastly, the Coldstream Guards, who specialise in reconnaissance operations, served in the Gulf War.

Made up of elite soldiers, the regiment is gradually beginning to embrace diversity. In 2007 sublieutenant Folarin Adeyemi Olatokunbo Olugbemiga Kuku became the first Black officer to join the Grenadier Guards. Originally from Nigeria, he distinguished himself at the military academy of Sandhurst, where he rubbed shoulders with Prince William. 'As far as the guardsmen are concerned, my colour doesn't matter – but my rank garners respect,' he declared, open about his ambition: to be promoted one day to General.[55]

Ten years later, in 2017, a woman led the Queen's Guard for the very first time. On the 150th anniversary of Canadian independence, Captain Megan Couto, who had only just turned 24, led the 2nd battalion of Princess Patricia's Light Infantry. Although it was a Canadian regiment, invited to London especially for the occasion – Elizabeth II was also Queen of Canada – feminisation was forging ahead in Her Majesty's armies, too. In 2019 all British Army corps were finally open to women, including the infantry. At the time, the Ministry of Defence was reflecting on the uniforms new female recruits would wear; the following day, they would be on duty in front of Buckingham Palace and would march in honour of their sovereign during the traditional Trooping the Colour ceremony.

London   12 June 2006

GARDEN PARTY

For the Windsors, garden parties are an institution. They began under Queen Victoria's reign, in the 1860s, and were for a long time restricted to high society. Until the 1950s, they provided an opportunity for young ladies of the English aristocracy to be presented at court and make their debut in society. It was not until the 1960s that the Palace opened up to other strata of society. More recently, Buckingham Palace described the gatherings as an opportunity for the monarch to meet 'a large range of people from all backgrounds, each of whom has played a positive part in their community'. Every summer, Queen Elizabeth hosted four such parties: three at Buckingham Palace and one at Holyrood Palace, in Edinburgh, providing more than 30,000 people with the chance to meet her and the members of the royal family accompanying her that day. The dress code was simple: for women, a dress and a hat or fascinator; and for men, a suit and tie. Members of the military wore their uniform. On 11 July 2006 the Queen wore a green silk dress accompanied by a coat designed by her dressmaker Karl-Ludwig Rehse, and a hat by Philip Somerville.

Garden parties always began at 4 p.m. – when Her Majesty would make her entrance and the military band would strike up the national anthem – although guests were welcome to arrive from 3 p.m. onwards.

I MUST BE THE ONLY PERSON THAT ALWAYS WEARS A HAT.

Elizabeth II to Philip Somerville

The Queen followed a fixed route, which was different from that of her husband or her children and grandchildren, if they were present, giving her guests – who numbered over 8,000 – a better chance of seeing her. There was no chance of a selfie with Elizabeth II, however. The ushers, retired officers of the armed forces called upon to lend a hand for the occasion, were responsible for selecting a number of individuals to be presented to the Queen, making sure they chose a varied panel of guests. On pieces of card, they scribbled down key facts about these lucky individuals, so that they could be properly introduced. Armed with these precious cards, the Lord Chamberlain would break the ice. Once she had reached the end of her social marathon, sometimes in the rain, the Queen would settle down in one of the marquees put up on the palace lawns, where she was joined by the other members of the royal family attending that day. At 6 p.m. the Windsors finally took their leave and the guests were politely invited to do the same.

Each summer 40,000 sandwiches and pieces of cake were consumed during these four receptions. In the absence of champagne, there was a steady supply of tea – more than 27,000 cups. The Queen also organised some special garden parties to celebrate noteworthy events during her reign. In 1997, for example, to mark her fiftieth wedding anniversary, she invited other couples who were also celebrating their golden wedding anniversaries to attend. In 2006, the year of her eightieth birthday, a garden party for children was organised at Buckingham Palace. Famous guests included the bestselling author J.K. Rowling, as well as Winnie-the-Pooh and Noddy.

THE DUCHESS OF CORNWALL

'They have overcome … all kinds of terrible obstacles. They have come through and I'm very proud and wish them well. My son is home and dry with the woman he loves. Welcome to the winners' enclosure.'[56] Although the Queen did not attend Charles and Camilla's civil wedding ceremony on 9 April 2005, she was present at the blessing ceremony at St George's Chapel, Windsor. Her toast to the happy couple – given on a race day – spoke volumes about her sense of relief after years of scandal. Camilla Shand, formerly Mrs Parker Bowles, had finally joined the royal family. As well as the Duchess of Cornwall, by marrying Prince Charles she also became the new Princess of Wales.[57]

What could Camilla bring to the British monarchy, other than a bit of peace? 'Camilla is an impulsive person. She does not purport to be anything other than what she is. She is the age she is and has no issue with it,' explains her biographer Penny Junor, who insists that 'the Duchess and the Queen [got] on marvellously.'[58] One year on from their wedding, Charles and Camilla joined Elizabeth and Philip in Scotland for the Braemar Gathering. The event, which includes the caber toss and tug of war competitions, has been a staple part of the Windsors' calendar since Queen Victoria.

Wearing a plumed hat created by Frederick Fox, the Queen was photographed chuckling away with her son and daughter-in-law, the image of a warm, happy family, in stark contrast to the glacial clique described by Diana. With Camilla, Charles seems at peace. The family ties were strengthened by the fact that as Prince of Wales and Duchess of Cornwall, Charles and Camilla loved spending time at their second home, Birkhall – which Charles inherited in 2002, when the Queen Mother passed away. This beautiful estate is just 12 km (7½ miles) from Balmoral Castle, where Elizabeth and Philip spent their summers.

Diana's shadow still loomed large, however. In 2007, on the tenth anniversary of their mother's death, Princes William and Harry organised a huge concert at Wembley Stadium in north London, raising £1 million for charitable causes. There was also a church service, to which the entire royal family was invited, including Camilla. After a great deal of hesitation, she decided not to attend, explaining her reasons in the following statement: 'I'm very touched to have been invited by Prince William and Prince Harry to attend the thanksgiving service for their mother Diana, Princess of Wales. I accepted and wanted to support them, however, on reflection I believe my attendance could divert attention from the purpose of the occasion which is to focus on the life and service of Diana.'

It was a matter of great speculation whether Camilla would one day be queen. At the time of her marriage, Buckingham Palace put a stop to the discussion by announcing that when her husband ascended the throne, the Duchess of Cornwall would bear the title Princess Consort. In the event she is known as Queen Consort – presumably a decision for the King, and for him alone.

Braemar

2 September 2006

HATS OFF TO CARLA

S he did it! At 1.02 p.m. on 26 March 2008, Carla Bruni-Sarkozy, who had been France's First Lady for less than eight weeks, met the Queen, pulling off the perfect curtsey under the admiring gaze of her husband and of the French public, who were following the event on live television. The President's wife had not been too keen, but there was no getting out of it, especially since Madame Chirac, her senior, had herself knelt with such good grace. The result lived up to expectation. The tabloids, which that morning had still been reeling off all the old clichés about Carla with her clothes off – the legacy of her former modelling career – had nothing but praise for her the following day.

In the United Kingdom, state visits are a well-oiled machine. Paying attention to the smallest detail, the Queen made it a point of honour to treat her guests to the utmost luxury. The State Banquet, held at Windsor Castle or Buckingham Palace, is a prerequisite. For the President of France and his wife, the banquet took place at Windsor, where Queen Victoria once welcomed Louis Philippe of France. In the immense St George's Hall, the palace staff set up the mahogany table dating back to 1846. Measuring 53 m (174 ft) long, it can seat 160 people, and members of the royal household took two whole days to lay it.

That evening, 158 lucky souls sat down to celebrate the friendship between England and France. They were treated to fillet of brill, lamb noisette with assorted vegetables, and rhubarb tart with vanilla ice cream, all washed down with a Chassagne-Montrachet 2000 and a Château-Margaux 1961. As was traditional, Her Majesty's chef presented his suggestions several months in advance. The Queen had the final word, however. Traditionally made up of four courses – although fourteen were commonly served under Queen Victoria and King Edward VII – the menus were described in the language of Molière, since French gastronomy had always been a point of reference. The Queen's grandfather George V employed a French cook, Henri Cédard, who presided over the royal kitchens from 1910 to 1935. In charge of a team of 80, he was constantly coming up with new recipes – no mean feat given that the King had a particular fondness for topside and veal tongue. For little Lilibet, the future Elizabeth II, he made incredible birthday cakes in the form of *bombes glacées*. The Queen was not known for her sweet tooth, though, much preferring a good Irish stew to pastries and cakes.

One year after the Sarkozys' visit, the British people had completely forgotten the hat the Queen wore to welcome the French President and First Lady: a bold creation adorned with feathers, designed by her dresser Angela Kelly. Carla's headpiece, on the other hand – a Christian Dior pillbox hat in the style of Jackie Kennedy – earned her first place that year on the Celebrity Hat Wearers list produced by the milliners of Luton, a small town in Bedfordshire that has been well known for its hat-making industry since the 19th century. Queen Elizabeth II had to settle for second place.

BACK TO THE EMIRATES

Abu Dhabi
24 November 2010

Featuring 82 domes, 4 minarets 106 m (350 ft) high, and 4,000 columns, the Sheikh Zayed Grand Mosque – one of the largest mosques in the world – is a dizzying sight. Elizabeth II discovered it for the first time on 24 November 2010, alongside Prince Philip and their son Prince Andrew. They were taken to see the mosque straight after landing, while on a five-day tour of the United Arab Emirates. The Queen's first official engagement involved a moment of meditation at the tomb of Zayed ben Sultan Al Nahyane, the founding father of the Emirates, who had welcomed her in 1979, during her first visit. Back then – in another era – the Queen had flown to Kuwait on Concorde before continuing her journey on board the royal yacht *Britannia*. Before entering the mosque, Elizabeth II had to take off her shoes. Officials had installed screens so that she felt more at ease, hidden from view. She also wore a long coat that covered her legs, designed by Angela Kelly, who accompanied her. The Queen's dresser had tied a golden scarf on top of her white pillbox hat.

The Queen came back out and was reunited with her hosts. 'This visit by the Head of the Church of England to the Sheikh Zayed Grand Mosque reflects the multidenominational dialogue and spirit of tolerance shared by the United Arab Emirates and

180
—
181

the United Kingdom,' Her Majesty's ambassador declared. Deeply religious, the Queen had always taken a particular interest in places of worship, of all forms. She was particularly fascinated by the mosques of the countries she visited, starting with her trip in 1961 to Pakistan, where she saw the Badshahi Mosque. It was not until 2002, however, that she visited a mosque in Great Britain, even though, according to some genealogists, she was a descendent of the Prophet Muhammad. She was said to owe such ancestry – which is fanciful, to say the least – to a certain Zaida of Seville, an 11th-century Muslim princess who converted to Catholicism in order to marry King Alfonso VI of Castile.

After Abu Dhabi, the Queen set off for Oman. There, too, significant changes had taken place over the previous 30 years. In 1979 the sultanate had just three schools and 15 km (9 miles) of paved roads. Sultan Qaboos bin Said Al Said, a great friend of the United Kingdom, transformed his country despite it being one of the emirates with the lowest supplies of oil. At the geopolitical level, the stability of Oman, which shares a border with Yemen, is vital. Qaboos, who had garnered a great deal of respect both within the region and further afield, was a skilled diplomat capable of negotiating at once with Israel, the United States and Iran. Elizabeth was visibly delighted to be reunited with the great sage, and the two chatted away in front of the photographers. As a token of friendship, the Sultan presented the Queen with an engraved gold vase and a Fabergé egg. Elizabeth had not come empty-handed, however. In return, she presented the Sultan – an avid fan of watches and clocks – with a first edition of a book from 1776 on watch- and clockmaking, signed by its author, Alexander Cumming (who has gone down in history for patenting the flushing toilet).

Abu Dhabi   24 November 2010

ALL BETS ARE OFF!

A pril 2011. The British people were indulging in one of their favourite hobbies: betting. In the United Kingdom, people bet on almost everything, not just horses and sporting events, and the lives of the royal family are the subject of some surprising bets. A royal wedding – the long-awaited marriage of Prince William and Catherine Middleton – proved a windfall for bookmakers. Would Kate arrive at Westminster Abbey on time? Or would she do a runner and jilt William at the altar? (With odds of 66 to 1, fortunately very few people thought she would do that …)

One of the most popular bets concerned the colour of the Queen's hat. On 8 April, three weeks before the ceremony, blue was on top, with odds of 3 to 1, followed by violet, pink and finally cream. Wrong! When the gates of Buckingham Palace opened, the crowds caught sight of the Queen through the windows of the state Bentley transporting her to the Abbey – in a yellow hat. Angela Kelly and Stella McLaren had opted for a bright shade and a boater style, decorated with two silk crêpe roses and four velvet leaves. Although the sky was overcast, the Queen was radiant.

This latest 'wedding of the century', as journalists dubbed it, was a source of great delight for the Windsors. The bride, nicknamed 'Waity Katie' on

184
—
185

account of her patience (she held on nine years for William to propose) – ticked all the boxes. Although a commoner (Diana had been an aristocrat), she came from a well-off family; her parents had made their fortune selling party supplies. The Middletons, who had had the good sense to enrol their daughter at the University of St Andrews, the establishment William also chose for his studies, adopted the customs of the aristocracy. Carole Middleton, Kate's mother, loves horse racing and can frequently be seen at Ascot, despite being the granddaughter of a miner and the daughter of a lorry driver. She is a self-made woman who earned the Queen's respect, just like her daughter: an incredible example of social advancement.

On 29 April 2011, in front of 1,900 guests, Catherine Elizabeth – you could not make it up – said 'yes' to her prince in a gown designed by Sarah Burton for Alexander McQueen. She wore a Cartier tiara made in 1936, loaned to her by the Queen for the occasion. By way of a wedding gift, the bride and groom received the titles of Duke and Duchess of Cambridge, Count and Countess of Strathearn, and Baron and Baroness Carrickfergus. When they left Westminster Abbey, Kate and William got into the landau that Charles and Diana had taken when they left St Paul's Cathedral after their wedding. Catherine had also received Diana's engagement ring, a Ceylon sapphire. And she happily went along with the ritual initiated by the Prince and Princess of Wales in 1981: a kiss on the palace balcony. The audience got their money's worth, however, as the newlyweds actually exchanged two.

London   29 April 2011

A RETURN TO PEACE

'One small step for ma'am, one giant leap for British-Irish relations.' These are the words Mark Simpson, the BBC's Dublin correspondent, used to sum up the general mood when Queen Elizabeth II set foot in the Republic of Ireland for the first time ever. Sure enough, the Queen was wearing green, even if she had opted for jade rather than an emerald shade. Her coat, made by the dressmaker Stewart Parvin, and hat, by the milliner Rachel Trevor-Morgan, were charming tributes to the Irish people, almost a declaration of love. Who would have thought it after the years of violence and countless bloody events seared into people's memories, such as the Bloody Sunday massacre of 1972 or the assassination of Lord Mountbatten (dear Uncle Dickie) by the IRA in August 1979? British-Irish relations had finally begun to warm.

The Queen was the first British sovereign to visit Dublin in a century, the last being her grandparents King George V and Queen Mary in July 1911, just two weeks after their coronation. At the time of that earlier visit the island, which had been under British rule since the 15th century and was the site of frequent revolts, longed for autonomy. A separatist party emerged in 1905. In this context, the arrival of the 'British King' hardly divided the crowds, at least if the daily newspaper the

Cork Examiner is to believed. The paper described the welcome extended to the royal couple and their two elder children, the Prince of Wales – later King Edward VIII – and Princess Mary, as 'cordial in the extreme'. Their Majesties nonetheless went out of their way to present the Irish people with the perfect image of a royal family full of promise, and to preserve the unity of an empire that was beginning to break apart. In quasi-tropical temperatures of 43°C (110°F), the King, who wore his admiral's uniform, and the Queen, dressed in a turquoise satin dress and a white toque hat decorated with ostrich feathers, waved with all their might. The local authorities feared a serious incident.

Symbolising the return to peace, Elizabeth II's visit elicited far more enthusiasm and praise in the press on both sides of the Irish Sea, even if it did trigger its fair share of hostile reactions and demonstrations, and called for unparalleled levels of security. Through an abundant demonstration of goodwill, the 'English Queen' disarmed countless opponents. At the Garden of Remembrance, created in the centre of Dublin in memory of those who had fought for the cause of Irish freedom, she bowed her head in respect. At the State Banquet, she impressed the assembly by beginning her speech in Gaelic, to the great astonishment of the President of Ireland, Mary McAleese. She returned to her native English, however, to express what sounded like a royal apology, regretting '[those] things which we would wish had been done differently or not at all'.

Dublin   17 May 2011

DEAREST OBAMAS

Barack Obama undeniably holds a special place in the long list of American presidents who have rubbed shoulders with the British royal family, as does his wife, Michelle. From their very first encounter, the Obamas and the Windsors hit it off. Had they not been wary of upsetting the Trump administration and sending a political signal to the world, Prince Harry and Meghan Markle would even have invited Barack and Michelle to their wedding on 19 May 2018.

The Obamas first visited Buckingham Palace in April 2009, after the G20 summit. In her autobiography *Becoming* (2018), in which she recounts her experiences as First Lady, Michelle describes this first meeting: 'The Queen kindly asked if we were suffering badly from jetlag and invited us to sit down … She looked me in the eye and asked me a few questions. She was warm and friendly, and I did my best to be equally friendly back.' A few hours later, however, the First Lady committed her first faux pas, during a reception for the G20 leaders. While talking to the Queen, Michelle placed a hand on the sovereign's back, in a typically American gesture. It did not matter if the Queen went on to perform a similar gesture in return; the damage was done. One does not touch Her Majesty. 'It was just a human gesture. I don't think it bothered the Queen,' Michelle noted.

In late May 2011 the couple returned to London for a two-day state visit during which the President of the United States was invited to deliver a speech to Parliament in Westminster Hall. The Obamas were again welcomed to Buckingham Palace. The Prince of Wales and the Duchess of Cornwall even made the journey from Clarence House for the occasion. Elizabeth II and Barack Obama inspected the 1st Battalion Scots Guards. Strong winds swept the First Lady's hair out of place and threatened to blow up her dress; the Queen had to clutch her own hat. 'Where is Michelle Obama's hat?', asked the American channel CBS. That evening, it was the President's turn to commit a faux pas. During the traditional banquet laid on in his honour, he proposed a toast just as the orchestra was striking up the national anthem. The audience, who had got to their feet for the anthem, were horror-struck. Tactfully, as the final notes of 'God Save the Queen' were sounding, Elizabeth II raised her glass as though nothing had happened, putting the President out of his misery.

'I really like the Queen,' he told his adviser, Ben Rhodes, that evening. 'She's like my grandmother. Courteous, direct; she says what she thinks. She won't stand for imbeciles.' Rhodes responded that the British Empire had been in decline for a long time, to which the American President responded, laughing: 'Well, they've got some wonderful relics! Did you see the Queen's diamonds?'[59]

London   24 May 2011

AN INVINCIBLE ARMADA

I n 2012 Elizabeth II celebrated the sixtieth anniversary of her accession to the throne. Before her, only her noble ancestor Queen Victoria had been fortunate enough to celebrate a diamond jubilee. On 22 June 1897, on a gloriously sunny day, the 'Grandmother of Europe' paraded through London, which was decked out with flags and bunting. More than a century later her great-great-granddaughter had to contend with rain.

It would take a lot more than temperatures of 12°C (54°F) to put off the British people, however, especially given the incredible sight to be seen: instead of the traditional promenade in a landau or coach, the Queen and her family treated themselves to a cruise on the River Thames aboard the *Spirit of Chartwell*, a cruise ship that had been revamped to resemble the royal barges of the 18th century. From Battersea Park to Tower Bridge, the ship was escorted by more than a thousand boats of all types: gondolas, Viking drakkars, Maori dugouts and canoes of all sizes. The parade was more akin to a carnival flotilla than an Invincible Armada.

As both the main attraction and a spectator herself, the Queen chose to set aside for a few hours the boater-cloche hats she had been wearing since the 2000s, and try something different. Drawing inspiration

198
—
199

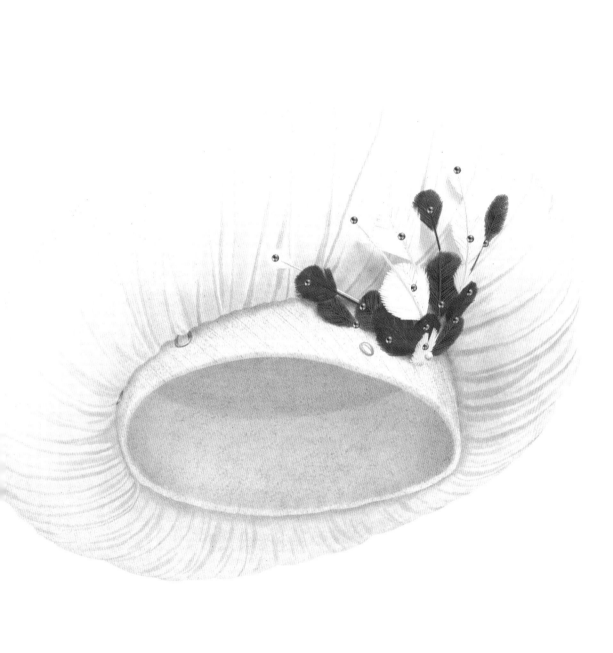

from the sumptuous costumes of the 16th century – another Elizabethan golden age – Angela Kelly and Stella McLaren made her a hat with a sloping brim, lined with silk jersey and adorned with feathers and rhinestones. The moment she finally placed it on her head marked the culmination of two years of work.

As impressive as it was, however, the Diamond Jubilee celebrations were not limited to the Thames Pageant. There was also a concert outside Buckingham Palace, a service of thanksgiving at St Paul's Cathedral, an air show and street parties galore. The festivities proved a boost for the tourism sector, which was gearing up for a record-breaking year with the Olympic Games in London.

The Queen's popularity – was she not the best-known woman in the world? – had also been a key factor in the International Olympic Committee's decision to hold the Games in the United Kingdom. For the opening ceremony, she played herself in a short film starring Daniel Craig as James Bond. Nine hundred million viewers burst into applause. The years of unpopularity were behind them: Windsor had become a global brand, with the Queen as its standard-bearer.

The royal family was sweeping the world off its feet once again, and not only among the new generation. A study by the University of Warwick revealed that Elizabeth II was a powerful marketing tool in China. For one in four Chinese people, she was the emblem of the United Kingdom, beating Big Ben and the Tower of London by a long way; 57 per cent even conceded that seeing her image on a product made them want to pull out their wallets. It is hardly surprising, then, that mugs with her face on them flew off the shelves, as did the commemorative biscuit tins featuring the royal coat of arms, sold at the Buckingham Palace shop and online. The British monarchy has become a lucrative industry, and the sale of souvenirs alone brings in over €20 million every year for the institution.

London 3 June 2012

THE LILAC REVOLUTION

The Queen wore black only on very rare occasions: for funerals; on Remembrance Sunday; and while visiting the Pope at the Vatican. That was the case until the early 2000s, at least.

Elizabeth II met five popes during her lifetime: Pius XII in 1951, when she was Princess; John XXIII in 1961; John Paul II on three occasions, in 1980, 1982 and 2000; Benedict XVI in 2010 (in London); and Francis in 2014. When she met Pope Francis, it was the first time the Queen had set foot in the Vatican for 14 years: an eternity for fashionistas. Here was an opportunity for a little sartorial revolution. Her Majesty had worn black for each of her visits since 1951, adhering scrupulously to tradition. As the colour of piety, black was the appropriate choice. His Holiness's protocol services also strongly recommended long sleeves, a mantilla and a stand-up collar. Only sovereigns and Catholic princesses have 'the privilege of wearing white' and can attend an audience with the Pope dressed all in white: the Queen of Spain; the Queen of Belgium; the Grand Duchess of Luxembourg; the Princess of Monaco; and the Princess of Naples, wife of the head of the House of Savoy and pretender to the Italian throne. Even though she is Catholic herself, Queen Máxima of the Netherlands is not permitted to wear white, because she is the wife of a Protestant sovereign. Elizabeth II was not only

WHAT POSSESSED THE QUEEN TO APPEAR BEFORE POPE FRANCIS WEARING A LILAC OUTFIT?

Protestant: she was the Supreme Governor of the Church of England.

What possessed her, then, to appear before Pope Francis on 3 April 2014 wearing a lilac outfit, with no mantilla, and a 'simple' stitched straw hat decorated with silk flowers? Although this was officially a private audience, there was in fact nothing private about the meeting, which was immortalised by photographers. Was the schedule too packed? Elizabeth II and Prince Philip had arrived in Rome in the morning and left that same evening. They had just come out from a luncheon with President Giorgio Napolitano; it is hard to imagine the Queen making conversation over the dinner table wearing a mantilla in view of her audience with the Pope in the afternoon. It is even harder to imagine her getting changed at the Palazzo del Quirinale, the Italian President's official residence. Pragmatism – and modesty – prevailed.

Pope Francis had ushered in a wind of change for the Church. For the journalist Joanna Moorhead, this lilac ensemble represented a positive step forward for women: 'Pope Francis was telling us that, in his world, if not in the weird Vatican world around him, women are "normal" and can look and behave normally around him.'[60] Women no longer had to drape themselves in black, as they had in the past. Camilla, Duchess of Cornwall, had clearly caught on when she visited Pope Francis in 2017 wearing a cream ensemble and no hat: cream, but not white, so as not to offend anyone who still held that privilege dear.

The Vatican   3 April 2014

LA VIE EN ROSE

For the opening of the flower market on the Île de la Cité in Paris, renamed the 'Marché aux fleurs Elizabeth-II' in her honour, the Queen wore a hat embellished with a rose, designed by Angela Kelly and made by Stella McLaren. Whether this was a thoughtful gesture or merely coincidence, the Parisians were won over once again. On 7 June 2014 the Queen began a three-day state visit to France, the fifth in her 62-year reign so far. The florists to whom she was introduced showered her with camellias, hydrangeas and orchids. One of them had even spared a thought for Prince Philip, her indefatigable companion. He presented the Prince with an eau de toilette by Fragonard (one of the oldest perfumeries from the famous town of Grasse), a nice touch that earned the florist a few words from Elizabeth II herself, and even a secret: the Queen did not have a favourite flower; she liked them all.

For the Windsors, flowers are a family affair. Members of the royal family have been loyal frequenters of the Chelsea Flower Show in London since Queen Mary in 1916. The show in 1937, the year of Elizabeth's parents' coronation, was particularly special. With pines from Canada, gladioli from Kenya and acacias from Australia, it was a true celebration of the Empire. Elizabeth II certainly inherited the family passion,

and King Charles is considered one of the greatest gardeners in the kingdom, having turned his residence at Highgrove in Gloucestershire into one of the most celebrated parks in the country. The Mayor of Paris, Anne Hidalgo, had made a wise move in naming the flower market after the Queen.

At 88 years of age, Elizabeth II joined her glorious predecessors in having her name immortalised on the capital's enamel signs, alongside Avenue Victoria, Place Édouard-VII, Avenue George-V and so on. Only her father was overlooked, although Winston Churchill had the honour. No one considered naming a road after her uncle, the scandalous Edward VIII, however. The city council had done enough for him by letting him rent for a modest sum the sublime private mansion on the edge of the Bois du Boulogne where he lived with his wife until his death. The tribute to the Queen was all the more meaningful on account of its being granted during her lifetime, an extremely rare occurrence. At the Paris Council, a number of councillors sought to oppose the initiative. On the far left, notably, some took umbrage at the fact that not even Robespierre had been granted such an honour. The cries of 'Vive la reine!' (Long live the Queen!) as Elizabeth passed by must have made the revolutionaries of 1792 turn in their graves …

If Paris presented Elizabeth II with a flower market, however, she had not come empty-handed herself. Alongside President François Hollande and the Mayor, the Queen unveiled a monumental sculpture on the Île de la Cité by the artist Diane Maclean. Over 2 m (6½ ft) high and made of stainless steel, the sculpture represents an open book. It was a gift that symbolised the future – yet to be written – of Franco-British relations. *Open Book* was installed in Martin Luther King Park in 2015, in the heart of the Batignolles district of Paris.

AN ANTI-BREXIT HAT?

London
17 June 2017

Was the Queen wearing the European flag on her head? On 17 June 2017, in the middle of the Brexit crisis, one year after Eurosceptics had won the referendum, the world wondered. Elizabeth II opened Parliament wearing a blue hat dotted with yellow beaded flowers that bore a striking resemblance to the stars of the European Union. This wasn't just a hat; it was a flag bearer. The media deliberated endlessly about this somewhat curious choice: 'Was it a deeply coded outfit, or simply Instagram-friendly? Was she throwing shade at the Brexit negotiations or referencing Van Gogh's *Starry Night*? Is this royal purple or Lanvin lilac?', pondered *The Guardian*.[61] Rarely had a sartorial choice by the monarch sent those in positions of power into such a frenzy.

Of course, the context made it difficult for people – who were already worked up – to see straight. The United Kingdom's painful exit from the European Union had turned the lives of the institutions upside down. Prime Minister Theresa May called for a snap election. On 8 June the British people cast their ballots, and on 17 June the Queen had to open an emergency session of Parliament, even though such an event – one of the most important engagements on her schedule every year – usually required weeks of planning. Under these conditions,

210
—
211

and under such tight time constraints, it would have been impossible to pull off the meticulous pageantry of a ceremony that had remained almost unchanged since 1852. Elizabeth II did not wear the state robe – a crimson velvet and ermine cloak 4.3 m (14 ft) long – or the Imperial State Crown, and her horse-drawn coach stayed at the stables. For the first time since 1974, when Harold Wilson of the Labour Party had made his return after winning a snap election, everything was stripped down to the bare bones. Back in 1974, the Queen had opened Parliament without her crown, a decision she found herself repeating 43 years later.

Why this hat, then? Was it a political message or simply a coincidence? Angela Kelly, the Queen's dresser, put a stop to the speculation in 2019: 'I already had some fabrics in stock to make Her Majesty's outfit. After checking where she would be standing, and making sure the colours wouldn't clash, I made a sketch and sent it to the Palace seamstress along with my instructions. Then, the milliner Stella McLaren and I sat down over a cup of tea to discuss the hat. We chose a style with an inverted rim so that Her Majesty's face would be clearly visible and so she herself would be able to see everyone … Neither Stella nor I ever imagined people would think we were copying the European flag.'[62] Nonetheless, the blue hat did not survive the media storm. The yellow beaded flowers were subsequently replaced with a large, reassuring ribbon, incapable of provoking even the slightest controversy.

London   17 June 2017

FIRST SOLO OUTING WITH MEGHAN

O n 14 June 2018, less than four weeks after her marriage to Prince Harry, Meghan Markle, the newly titled Duchess of Sussex, accompanied Elizabeth II on an outing to Chester, in the north of England. It was a huge honour to be invited on a solo outing with the Queen (Kate had had to wait eight years), but in the face of the new Duchess's incredible popularity, how could she resist? Meghan and Harry's wedding had been followed on television by two billion viewers. The newest recruit to the 'Firm' was a hit, especially among the younger generations, who were far less receptive to the Windsors' stilted splendour. As well as providing a chance to showcase Elizabeth's genuine fondness for her grandson's wife, the outing was also a wonderful public-relations operation. Meghan was even invited to travel on the royal train, previously reserved only for the Queen, Prince Philip, Prince Charles and his wife, Camilla: a sure-fire way to trigger tension and unleash burgeoning jealousy …

The Queen and the Duchess of Sussex left London the evening before. After dinner the train stopped on a dedicated track to allow the passengers to sleep in complete peace and quiet. They reached their destination the following morning, and were greeted at the station by the authorities. The Queen got out

214
—
215

WHEN I ARRIVED IN LONDON THERE WERE WAY TOO MANY FLOWERS ON THE HATS!

Marie O'Regan

first. She was wearing a bright green coat designed by Stewart Parvin and a matching hat by Rachel Trevor-Morgan. It was not a new outfit; she had worn it for the commemoration of the 70th anniversary of the D-Day landings on 6 June 2014, in Ouistreham, Normandy. On this occasion, however, the colour was seen as a tribute to the 72 victims of the Grenfell Tower fire on 14 June 2017. One year later, to the day, the British people wore green in memory of the tragic event.

Meghan Markle, for her part, opted for a grey dress by the French fashion house Givenchy, which had also designed her wedding gown. She did not wear a hat, perhaps as a way of asserting her difference. The outing was nonetheless a great success. The two women showed a united front throughout the day, and the Duchess of Sussex did not put a foot wrong. She simply hesitated a little when getting into the car with the Queen, seeming unsure which seat to take. 'Which would you prefer?', she asked simply. 'You go first,' replied an amused Elizabeth II.

Who would have thought, then, that a year and a half later, the rising star of the monarchy, fed up with the tabloids' constant attacks and perhaps with royal life itself, would choose to throw in the towel? And yet …

Chester   14 June 2018

THE ORDER OF THE GARTER

I n 1348 King Edward III of England was savouring his victories. His troops had crushed the French at Crécy and had just taken Calais after an 11-month siege (the town remained under English rule for more than two centuries, until 1558). The Hundred Years War was clearly turning to England's advantage. Flushed with success, the King resolved to set up a new chivalric order, inspired by Arthurian tradition. Legend has it that it was an amorous mishap that provided him with the opportunity. During a ball, his mistress, the Countess of Salisbury, lost her garter while dancing. The poor lady was the laughing stock of the court. Gallantly, Edward picked up the ribbon and tied it around his calf: 'Honni soit qui mal y pense' ('Shamed be whoever thinks ill of it'). The same people who had laughed at the hapless countess were now fighting to imitate the King and be distinguished by him, and the Order of the Garter was born.

In 1948 George VI – the hero of another war – set about returning this order, the oldest in Britain, to its former glory. To mark its 600th anniversary, he organised a lavish ceremony – the likes of which had not been seen for more than a century – at Windsor Castle. The King took the opportunity to present the insignia of the Garter to his son-in-law Philip, and to make

his daughter Elizabeth a 'noblewoman'. Determined to uphold her father's legacy, Elizabeth II kept the tradition alive by continuing to invite the members of the order to Windsor every spring. For it was up to the sovereign to select the members – who originally numbered no more than 24 – honouring people from all backgrounds for their commitment and service to the nation, as well as members of her own family, such as Princess Anne, Prince William and Prince Edward.

On 17 June 2019 Her Majesty prepared to officially install two kings as Knights of the Garter: Felipe VI of Spain and Willem-Alexander of the Netherlands. They had been appointed during state visits to Britain in 2017 and 2018, respectively. Duly installed, Spain and the Netherlands walked in procession alongside their new companions in arms, just as George VI and his own kith and kin had done in 1948. The only departure from tradition during this joyful procession, which tourists watched with delight, was that the Queen arrived in the State Bentley, on account of her age. The Sovereign of the Garter wore the traditional dress of the order: a midnight-blue velvet robe and a hat in the style of a Tudor bonnet, trimmed with a white ostrich plume. It was a far cry from the woollen tunic and hood worn by Edward III's first knights.

The kings of Spain and the Netherlands are not the only foreign sovereigns to have been honoured by Elizabeth II. To cite just a few, Queen Margrethe II of Denmark, King Carl XVI Gustaf of Sweden, King Juan Carlos of Spain and King Harald V of Norway all preceded them in receiving the honour. But that honour can also very easily be taken away. This is what happened to the Emperor of Austria, Franz Josef, and the Emperor of Germany, Wilhelm II, both of whom were dismissed by George V in 1915 for joining the opposing camp. Emperor Hirohito of Japan, on the other hand, who became a Knight of the Order of the Garter in 1929, became *persona non grata* during the Second World War before rejoining the order in 1971, at the decision of the Queen.

Windsor   17 June 2019

THE NATION'S HERO

H er Majesty made her way across the courtyard of Windsor Castle at her own pace, to the sound of bagpipes. Captain Tom Moore stood waiting for her, leaning on his famous walking frame. Having just turned 100, right in the middle of the Covid-19 pandemic, this former officer of the British Army – who had served in India and Burma and now struggled to walk – had been a national hero for a few months. On 6 April 2020, four weeks before his hundredth birthday, he had set himself a challenge: to complete 100 laps of his 25 m (82 ft) garden. It was a remarkable feat for the veteran, who immediately set up an online fundraising page to help support health workers.

At the time, Captain Tom hoped to raise £1,000, but the social networks and the media quickly got hold of the story and he became a national idol. The challenge caused such a stir that he reached his initial target in just four days. The process had been set in motion, and the dashing walker – who had the whole country behind him – was not going to stop there. He went on to raise more than £32 million. Following a proposal by Prime Minister Boris Johnson, the decision was taken to knight him. And so, on 17 July 2020, carrying the sword of her father, King George VI, Queen Elizabeth was visibly delighted to do the honours by awarding him his knighthood.

COLOUR IS PARAMOUNT.

Angela Kelly

For the occasion, the Queen chose a mint-green coat and a floral dress. She also wore a new hat: a stitched straw and wool crêpe creation in the same shade, designed by Angela Kelly and made by Stella McLaren. The headpiece was crowned with leaves and flowers, also made of straw, as well as understated grey feathers shaped like arrows. After all, when it comes to honouring a great man, nothing is too beautiful. The Queen's hat was not chosen for the captain's eyes alone, however. She had in fact begun her day by attending the wedding of her granddaughter Princess Beatrice of York to Edoardo Mapelli Mozzi, which was carried out in the utmost secrecy – a first in 235 years for the royal family – blindsiding fans all over the world. It had been a marathon of a day, as she told Sir Tom: 'My granddaughter got married this morning. Philip and I managed to get there – very nice.'

The public had to wait until the next day before a select few pictures of the wedding were released. The newlyweds could be seen beaming as they left the Royal Chapel of All Saints, near Windsor Castle. They posed for the cameras alongside the Queen, who was wearing the same hat, and Prince Philip. The pandemic had put a stop to the large wedding they had dreamed of, which was initially planned to take place on 29 May 2020. Fewer than 20 guests were able to attend the private ceremony. The bride was nonetheless determined to pay tribute to her grandmother by wearing one of her dresses, made by the British designer Norman Hartnell and worn by the Queen to open Parliament in 1967. The garment was a true piece of history, altered to fit the princess by the indispensable Angela Kelly.

WE'VE MISSED YOU

Because of the Covid-19 pandemic, she had not been out to meet her subjects for seven months. On 15 October 2020, however, the British people were finally reunited with their sovereign. After 220 days of self-isolation – which she split between Windsor, Balmoral and Sandringham – Elizabeth II made her first official outing, accompanied by her grandson Prince William. The pair visited a laboratory of the Ministry of Defence specialising in the fight against terrorism.

The nation was delighted: the Queen was wearing pink! Sporting a wide-brimmed floral headpiece, Her Majesty seemed relaxed and pleased to be back in touch with the public, where she was in her element. It was an opportunity to show that nothing could stop her, not even a global epidemic. 'Her Majesty The Queen's uplifting colourful ensembles are definitely on the list of things we have missed since lockdown began,' declared the *Evening Standard*. Even the ever-serious *Telegraph* saw things through rose-tinted glasses: 'With a knack for picking just the right lipstick to lift the nation, Her Majesty The Queen's pink make-up moment is a welcome sight.'[63] This was all the truer since Elizabeth, an expert in recycling – and communication – did not do things by halves; she had already worn the hat and coat in March 2019 for a visit to King's College

London, when she was accompanied by Kate. That was almost exactly a year before the country shut down. The monarchy was unshakable.

Why, though, was the Queen not wearing a mask as well as a hat? Had all the necessary precautions been taken to protect the Head of State, who, even if she was in robust health, was still 95 years old? Questioned by the press, Buckingham Palace explained its reasons. Nothing had been left to chance. On the ground, strict markings indicated where everyone could stand, in accordance with social distancing regulations. The laboratory staff had also been tested 'very recently', according to the Palace, as had Prince William. The general public later learned that William had contracted Covid-19 in April 2020, six months before the visit, as his father, Prince Charles, had in March. Lastly, the site itself had been chosen to guarantee the Queen's safety: an open-air building was selected over an enclosed space that would have had to be ventilated at all times. Elizabeth II arrived directly from Windsor by helicopter, to limit her contact with others, and left, again by air, after just 45 minutes. Be that as it may, the absence of a mask still left some dumbfounded.

In 2020 the Queen was seen wearing a mask just once: during a private ceremony held to pay tribute to the Unknown Warrior on 4 November, in Westminster Abbey. Face coverings were required by law in indoor settings, including places of worship. No matter that the Queen was practically alone in the enormous nave, accompanied only by the Dean of Westminster, Reverend David Hoyle, and her equerry, Lieutenant Colonel Nana Kofi Twumasi-Ankrah. The precedent was set.

FAREWELL, PHILIP

t 2.38 p.m. London time, the Duke of Edinburgh's coffin was hoisted on to the Land Rover he had designed himself for his funeral: the final gesture of an eccentric prince and insatiable all-rounder, who passed away at the age of 99. Behind the vehicle, which set off towards St George's Chapel, Windsor, walked his children (Prince Charles, Princess Anne, Prince Andrew and Prince Edward), three of his grandchildren (Prince William, Prince Harry and Peter Phillips), his son-in-law Timothy Laurence (Princess Anne's husband) and his nephew David Linley (Princess Margaret's son). They were followed by Philip's closest staff members: his personal protection officer, his private secretary, two pages and two valets. Elizabeth II brought up the rear in the State Bentley, accompanied by a lady-in-waiting. The Queen was burying the man of her life, her husband of 73 years. The United Kingdom and the Commonwealth, meanwhile, bid farewell to the man who held the record for the longest-serving prince consort.

Because of the pandemic, only 30 people could attend the ceremony in the chapel, all socially distanced. Elizabeth II sat alone in the pews, wearing a face covering. Stella McLaren had made her a hat with an upturned brim, very similar to the one she had worn for the funeral of Prince Philip's cousin

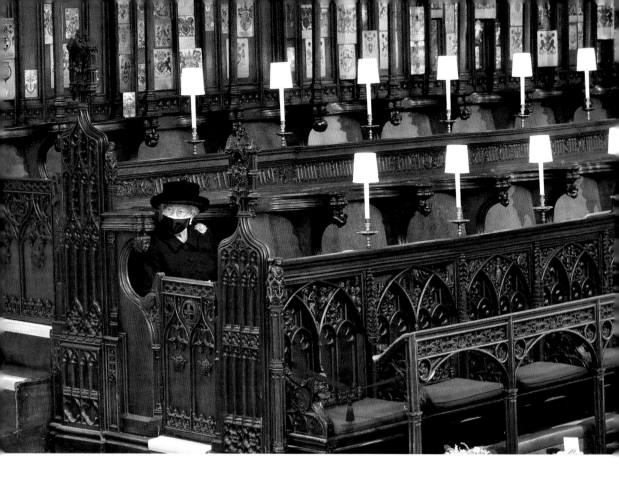

THE WORLD WOULD BARELY CATCH A GLIMPSE OF THE HAT: OUT OF RESPECT, THE BBC CAMERAS RESTED ON THE QUEEN, IN HER GRIEF, ONLY FOR A MOMENT.

Countess Mountbatten of Burma, who passed away in 2017. Rather than satin, the milliner chose to cover this headpiece with velvet. The world would barely catch a glimpse of the hat, however: out of respect, the BBC cameras rested on the Queen, in her grief, only for a moment. Viewers would have to settle for a glimpse of the sovereign; just days from turning 95, she deserved that.

Prince Philip had made it clear that he did not want a grand funeral like the one put on for the Queen Mother in 2002, or for Diana in 1997. Covid-19 had its own rules to impose. Although only his closest relatives could accompany him to his final resting place – the coffin was in fact placed in the royal crypt, to be transferred next to that of his wife when she should pass away – outside, more than 700 soldiers paid tribute to him. Before becoming Prince Consort, Philip Mountbatten, born Prince Philip of Greece and Denmark, had indeed been a war hero, one of the youngest officers of the Royal Navy. A selection of the 61 medals conferred on him were positioned on 9 cushions.

At the end of the ceremony, the Queen and her family took their leave. While Elizabeth got back into the family car, the rest of the family chose to walk. Prince Harry, who was on bad terms with the rest of the clan, walked next to his brother, Prince William. The Prince of Wales' two sons finally spoke to each other. Their short exchange seemed to provide some hope – which was quickly dashed – that the relationship might be repaired. Could the Windsors sort things out? Would they grow stronger? Would Charles prove up to the challenges that lay ahead of him? What was the future of the crown, which for 70 years had been worn by a woman who had woven her way tirelessly across the globe? A woman who would be remembered for her courage, her dignity and her sense of duty. And in every image, throughout every event – be it happy or sad – are her hats.

Windsor   17 April 2021

THE MILLINERS

1 – THE MODEL LITTLE GIRL
Smith & Co.

2 – THE CALL TO ARMS
Auxiliary Territorial Service (ATS)

3 – A LESSON IN STYLE
Aage Thaarup

4 – A PRINCESS IN PARIS
Aage Thaarup

5 – TROOPING THE COLOUR
Aage Thaarup

6 – MORE HATS FOR MISS DONALD
Aage Thaarup

7 – THE NEW YORK MARATHON
Aage Thaarup

8 – MARGARET GETS MARRIED
Claude Saint-Cyr or Simone Mirman

9 – THE CHARM AFTER THE STORM
Claude Saint-Cyr

10 – FLOWER POWER
Simone Mirman

11 – THE SPAGHETTI HAT
Simone Mirman

12 – UNCLE DICKIE
Aage Thaarup

13 – CROWNING CHARLES
Simone Mirman

14 – ONE STEP CLOSER TO THE PUBLIC
Simone Mirman

15 – THE DUKE OF WINDSOR QUIETLY PASSES AWAY
Frederick Fox or Simone Mirman

16 – HIGHCLERE
Simone Mirman

17 – THE CHRYSANTHEMUM THRONE
Simone Mirman

18 – TWO HATS FOR THE PRICE OF ONE
Frederick Fox and Simone Mirman

19 – THE LADIES OF THE BAHAMAS
Simone Mirman

20 – A HIGH-RISK MISSION
Simone Mirman

21 – A NIGHTMARE IN THE SUNSHINE
Simone Mirman

22 – THE WEDDING OF THE CENTURY
Simone Mirman

23 – WHO TRIED TO KILL THE QUEEN?
Marie O'Regan

24 – THE QUEEN ON THE OTHER SIDE OF THE WORLD
Frederick Fox

25 – CHARMING COMPANY
Valerie Lee

26 – MADE FOR CHINA
Frederick Fox

27 – THE TALKING HAT
Frederick Fox

28 – ANNUS HORRIBILIS
Frederick Fox

29 – THE MAGNUM OPUS
Marie O'Regan

30 – THE WORLD MOURNS DIANA
Frederick Fox

31 – END OF AN ERA
Marie O'Regan

32 – HAZARDS OF THE JOB
Marie O'Regan

33 – GREETINGS FROM NORWAY
Frederick Fox

34 – THE FUTURE IS IN SAFE HANDS
Philip Somerville

35 – GARDEN PARTY
Philip Somerville

36 – THE DUCHESS OF CORNWALL
Frederick Fox

37 – HATS OFF TO CARLA
Angela Kelly and Stella McLaren

38 – BACK TO THE EMIRATES
Angela Kelly and Stella McLaren

NOTES

39 – ALL BETS ARE OFF!
Angela Kelly and Stella McLaren

40 – A RETURN TO PEACE
Rachel Trevor-Morgan

41 – DEAREST OBAMAS
Angela Kelly and Stella McLaren

42 – AN INVINCIBLE ARMADA
Angela Kelly and Stella McLaren

43 – THE LILAC REVOLUTION
Rachel Trevor-Morgan

44 – LA VIE EN ROSE
Angela Kelly and Stella McLaren

45 – AN ANTI-BREXIT HAT?
Angela Kelly and Stella McLaren

46 – FIRST SOLO OUTING WITH MEGHAN
Rachel Trevor-Morgan

47 – THE ORDER OF THE GARTER
Ede & Ravenscroft

48 – THE NATION'S HERO
Angela Kelly and Stella McLaren

49 – WE'VE MISSED YOU
Rachel Trevor-Morgan

50 – FAREWELL, PHILIP
Angela Kelly and Stella McLaren

INTRODUCTION

1 – Jacqueline Demornex, *Le Siècle en chapeaux. Claude Saint-Cyr, histoire d'une modiste*, Éditions du May, 1991.

2 – Mabell Ogilvy, *Thatched with Gold: The Memoirs of Mabell, Countess of Airlie*, Hutchinson, 1962.

3 – *Londonderry Sentinel*, 11 April 1953.

4 – Aage Thaarup and Dora Shackell, *Heads and Tales: The Autobiography of Aage Thaarup*, Cassell & Co., 1956.

5 – Demornex, op. cit.

6 – Simone Mirman worked in conjunction with her husband, Serge Mirman, who designed eccentric hats intended to attract the attention of the press. In this way, the Mirmans guaranteed themselves wide publicity.

7 – *Daily Mirror*, 29 September 1965.

8 – Ian Thomas, interviewed in the *Evening Express* on 22 October 1976.

9 – *Liverpool Echo*, 14 September 1982.

10 – Angela Kelly, *The Other Side of the Coin: The Queen, the Dresser and the Wardrobe*, HarperCollins Publishers, 2019.

11 – Demornex, op. cit.

12 – Interview with the author, 25 February 2021.

13 – Frederick Fox and Linda Sandino, *An Oral History of British Fashion*, transcript of five interviews given at the British Library, National Life Story Collection, 2004.

14 – Interview with the author, 16 February 2021.

15 – Letter from Ian Thomas, undated, in Marie O'Regan's personal archive.

16 – Interview with Caroline de Guitaut, curator of the exhibition 'Fashioning a Reign: 90 Years of Style from the Queen's Wardrobe' (Royal Collection Trust, 2016), *The Telegraph*, 22 December 2016.

17 – Fox and Sandino, op. cit.

18 – Kelly, op. cit.

NOTES

19 – Fox and Sandino, op. cit.

20 – Quoted in Mike Southon, *The Millinery Lesson*, documentary film, Nodal Point Media, 2017.

21 – Interview with the author, 16 February 2021.

22 – Handwritten letter from Queen Elizabeth II to Philip Somerville, dated 25 February 2007, auctioned by Fraser's Autographs in London on 20 March 2015.

23 – Other dressmakers who worked with the Queen in the 1980s, 1990s and 2000s are John Anderson, Karl-Ludwig Rehse, Maureen Rose and Peter Enrione.

THE HATS

1 – Marion Crawford, *The Little Princesses: The Story of the Queen's Childhood by her Nanny*, Cassell & Co., 1950.

2 – Quoted in ibid.

3 – Ibid.

4 – Graham Viney, *The Last Hurrah: South Africa and the Royal Tour of 1947*, Jonathan Ball Publishers, 2018.

5 – Aage Thaarup and Dora Shackell, *Heads and Tales: The Autobiography of Aage Thaarup*, Cassell & Co., 1956.

6 – *France-Soir*, 15 May 1948.

7 – Anne Edwards, *The Queen's Clothes*, Express Newspapers & Elm Tree Books, 1976.

8 – *Ce Soir*, 14 May 1948.

9 – Thaarup and Shackell, op. cit.

10 – Ibid.

11 – *Life* magazine, 24 June 1957.

12 – Quoted in *Daily Mirror*, 22 October 1957.

13 – Quoted in Jacqueline Demornex, *Le Siècle en chapeaux. Claude Saint-Cyr, histoire d'une modiste*, Éditions du May, 1991.

14 – Ibid.

15 – *Daily Mirror*, 4 February 1961.

16 – *Reading Standard*, 23 June 1961.

17 – *Coventry Evening Telegraph*, 29 January 1960.

18 – *Reading Standard*, 23 June 1961.

19 – *Birmingham Post*, 18 January 1966.

20 – Interview with the author, 25 February 2021.

21 – *Daily Mirror*, 27 July 1965.

22 – *Daily Mirror*, 5 August 1965.

23 – Quoted in Alan Rosenthal, *The New Documentary in Action: A Casebook in Film Making*, University of California Press, 1971.

24 – Robert Lacey, *Monarch: The Life and Reign of Elizabeth II*, Free Press, 2002.

25 – Quoted in Hugo Vickers, *Behind Closed Doors: The Tragic, Untold Story of the Duchess of Windsor*, Hutchinson, 2011.

26 – Léon Zitrone, *Au bout de mes jumelles*, Buchet/Chastel, 1975.

27 – Quoted in Isabelle Rivère, *Elizabeth II, dans l'intimité du règne*, Fayard, 2020.

28 – Hugh Cortazzi, *Japan Experiences: Fifty Years, One Hundred Views, Post-War Japan through British Eyes, 1945–2000*, Japan Society Publications, 2001.

29 – Frederick Fox and Linda Sandino, *An Oral History of British Fashion*, transcript of five interviews given at the British Library, National Life Story Collection, 2004.

30 – Ibid.

31 – *Birmingham Post*, 3 August 1979.

32 – Quoted in the *Sunday Mirror*, 5 August 1979.

33 – Robert Hardman, *Our Queen*, Hutchinson, 2011.

34 – Quoted in the *Liverpool Echo*, 14 September 1982.

35 – Ibid.

36 – Letter of thanks to the Prime Minister of New Zealand, Robert Muldoon, dated 20 October 1981, signed by Prince Philip.

37 – *Liverpool Echo*, 15 October 1981.

38 – *The Guardian*, 13 January 2018.

BIBLIOGRAPHY

39 – Stanley Dalby, Taliu Eli and Don Murray, *Change in Tuvalu*, documentary film, Film Australia, 1983.

40 – *Daily Mirror*, 29 March 1984.

41 – *Sunday Mirror*, 1 April 1984.

42 – Ibid.

43 – *Evening Express*, 13 October 1986.

44 – Ibid.

45 – *Courier & Advertiser*, 15 October 1986.

46 – Fox and Sandino, op. cit.

47 – Robert Hardman, *Queen of the World*, Century, 2018.

48 – Nick Tanner, *The Queen's Worst Year*, documentary film, Nent Studios, 2016.

49 – Interview with the author, 16 February 2021.

50 – The second was part of the exhibition 'Fashioning a Reign: 90 Years of Style from the Queen's Wardrobe' in 2016.

51 – *Irish Independent*, 7 May 1994.

52 – *The Mirror*, 6 September 1997.

53 – Ibid.

54 – Angela Kelly, *The Other Side of the Coin: The Queen, the Dresser and the Wardrobe*, HarperCollins Publishers, 2019.

55 – *Le Monde*, 25 January 2007.

56 – Quoted in Isabelle Rivère, *Camilla & Charles*, Robert Laffont, 2004.

57 – Camilla is also Duchess of Rothesay, Countess of Chester, Countess of Carrick and Baroness of Renfrew.

58 – Penny Junor, *The Duchess: Camilla Parker Bowles and the Love Affair that Rocked the Crown*, HarperCollins Publishers, 2017.

59 – Ben Rhodes, *The World as It Is: Inside the Obama White House*, Random House, 2018.

60 – *The Guardian*, 4 April 2014.

61 – *The Guardian*, 21 June 2017.

62 – Kelly, op. cit.

63 – *Evening Standard*, 15 October 2020; *The Telegraph*, 15 October 2020.

AMPHLETT Hilda, *Hats: A History of Fashion in Headwear*, Dover Publications, 2003

ANDERSON Robert, *Fifty Hats that Changed the World*, The Design Museum/ Conran Octopus, 2011

BRICARD Isabelle, *Les Dynasties régnantes d'Europe*, Perrin, 2000

CORTAZZI Hugh, *Japan Experiences: Fifty Years, One Hundred Views, Post-War Japan through British Eyes, 1945–2000*, Japan Society Publications, 2001

CRAWFORD Marion, *The Little Princesses: The Story of the Queen's Childhood by her Nanny*, Cassell & Co., 1950

DEMORNEX Jacqueline, *Le Siècle en chapeaux. Claude Saint-Cyr, histoire d'une modiste*, Éditions du May, 1991

EDWARDS Anne, *The Queen's Clothes*, Express Newspapers & Elm Tree Books, 1976

GLENCONNER Anne, *Lady in Waiting: My Extraordinary Life in the Shadow of the Crown*, Hodder & Stoughton, 2019

HARDMAN Robert, *Our Queen*, Hutchinson, 2011

——, *Queen of the World*, Century, 2018

HARTNELL Norman, *Silver and Gold*, Evan Brothers, 1955

HOLMES Elizabeth, *HRH: So Many Thoughts on Royal Style*, Celadon Books, 2020

JONES Kathryn, *For the Royal Table: Dining at the Palace*, Royal Collection Trust, 2008

JUNOR Penny, *The Duchess: Camilla Parker Bowles and the Love Affair that Rocked the Crown*, HarperCollins Publishers, 2017

KELLY Angela, *Dressing the Queen: The Jubilee Wardrobe*, Royal Collection Trust, 2012

——, *The Other Side of the Coin: The Queen, the Dresser and the Wardrobe*, HarperCollins Publishers, 2019

BIBLIOGRAPHY

KIMPTON Peter, *Edwardian Ladies' Hat Fashions: 'Where Did You Get that Hat?'*, Pen and Sword Books, 2017

LACEY Robert, *Monarch: The Life and Reign of Elizabeth II*, Free Press, 2002

——, *A Brief Life of the Queen*, Duckworth Overlook, 2012

LE MAUX Nicole, *Histoire du chapeau féminin*, Charles Massin, 2000

MARSCHNER Joanna, BEHLEN Beatrice, *Hats and Handbags: Accessories from the Royal Wardrobe*, Kensington Palace, Historic Royal Palaces, 2003

MEYER-STABLEY Bertrand, *La Véritable Duchesse de Windsor*, Pygmalion, 2002

OBAMA Michelle, *Becoming*, Viking Press, 2018

OGILVY Mabell, *Thatched with Gold: The Memoirs of Mabell, Countess of Airlie*, Hutchinson, 1962

PEAT Rachel, *Japan: Courts and Culture*, Royal Collection Trust, 2020

PICK Michael, *Hardy Amies*, ACC Art Books, 2012

——, *Norman Hartnell: The Biography*, Zuleika Books & Publishing, 2019

PIGOTT Peter, *Royal Transport: An Inside Look at the History of Royal Travel*, Dundurn Press, 2005

RHODES Ben, *The World as It Is: Inside the Obama White House*, Random House, 2018

RHODES Margaret, *The Final Curtsey*, Umbria Press, 2011

RIVÈRE Isabelle, *Camilla & Charles*, Robert Laffont, 2004

——, *Elizabeth II, dans l'intimité du règne*, Fayard, 2020

SMITH Malcolm, *Hats: A Very Unnatural History*, Michigan State University Press, 2020

THAARUP Aage, SHACKELL Dora, *Heads and Tales: The Autobiography of Aage Thaarup*, Cassell & Co., 1956

VICKERS Hugo, *Behind Closed Doors: The Tragic, Untold Story of the Duchess of Windsor*, Hutchinson, 2011

VINEY Graham, *The Last Hurrah: South Africa and the Royal Tour of 1947*, Jonathan Ball Publishers, 2018

WILLIAMS Kate, *Young Elizabeth: The Making of Our Queen*, Weidenfeld & Nicolson, 2012

ZIEGLER Philip, *King Edward VIII: The Official Biography*, HarperCollins Publishers, 1991

ZITRONE Léon, *Au bout de mes jumelles*, Buchet/Chastel, 1975

CREDITS

p.3 © Anwar Hussein/Getty Images; p.7 © Fox Photos/Getty Images; p.9 © Keystone/Getty Images; p.10 © Bettman/Getty Images; p.12 TL © Archives Marie O'Regan; p.12 TR & BL © Tim Graham Photo Library via Getty Images; p.12 BR © Ray Bellisario/Popperfoto via Getty Images/Getty Images; p.13 © Tim Graham Photo Library via Getty Images; p.15 TL © Chris Jackson/Getty Images; p.15 TR © Serge Lemoine/Getty Images; p.15 BL & BR © Tim Graham Photo Library via Getty Images; p.16 © Tristan Fewings/BFC/Getty Images; pp.18–19 © *Daily Mirror*/Mirrorpix/Mirrorpix via Getty Images; p.21 © Scott Barbour/Getty Images/AFP; p.24 © Hulton-Deutsch Collection/CORBIS/Corbis via Getty Images; p.28 © Popperfoto via Getty Images/Getty Images; p.32 © Rolls Press/Popperfoto via Getty Images/Getty Images; p.36 © KEYSTONE-France/Gamma- Rapho via Getty Images; p.40 © Bettman/Getty Images; p.44 © Popperfoto via Getty Images/Getty Images; p.48 © Ben Martin/Getty Images; pp.50–51 © Popperfoto via Getty Images/Getty Images;

ACKNOWLEDGEMENTS

p.54 © Loomis Dean/The LIFE Picture Collection/Getty Images; p.58 © Popperfoto via Getty Images/Getty Images; pp.60–61 © Hulton-Deutsch Collection/CORBIS/Corbis via Getty Images; p.64 © Ray Bellisario/Popperfoto via Getty Images/Getty Images; p.68 © Kurt Rohwedder/picture alliance via Getty Images; p.72 © Fox Photos/Getty Images; p.76 © Hulton Archive/Getty Images; p.80 © Keystone/Hulton Archive/Getty Images; p.84 © Hulton Archive/Getty Images; p.88 © Michel GINFRAY/Gamma-Rapho via Getty Images; p.92 © Nik Wheeler/Corbis via Getty Images; p.94–5 © The Asahi Shimbun via Getty Images; p.98 © Popperfoto via Getty Images/Getty Images; pp.102, 106 © Anwar Hussein/Getty Images; p.110 © Francis Apesteguy/Getty Images; p.114 © Tim Graham Photo Library via Getty Images; pp.118, 122 © Anwar Hussein/Getty Images; p.126 © Popperfoto via Getty Images/Getty Images; pp.130, 134, 136–7, 140, 144 © Graham Photo Library via Getty Images; pp.146–7 © Pool Bassignac/Gaillarde/Simon/Gamma-Rapho via Getty Images; p.150 © John Shelley Collection/Avalon/Getty Images; pp.154, 158 © Tim Graham Photo Library via Getty Images; p.162 © John Shelley Collection/Avalon/Getty Images; p.166 © Anwar Hussein Collection/ROTA/WireImage; p.170 © Mark Cuthbert/UK Press via Getty Images; p.174 © Anwar Hussein Collection/ROTA/WireImage; p.178 © Pool Interagences/Gamma-Rapho via Getty Images; pp.182, 186 © Chris Jackson/Getty Images; pp.188–9 © Paul Cunningham/Corbis via Getty Images; p.192 © Samir Hussein/WireImage/Getty Images; p.196 © Rota/Anwar Hussein/Getty Images; p.200 © Mark Cuthbert/UK Press via Getty Images; p.203–4 © Vatican Pool/Getty Images; p.208 © Chris Jackson/Getty Images; p.212 © Carl Court/Getty Images/AFP; p.216 © Mark Cuthbert/UK Press via Getty Images; p.220 © Patrick van Katwijk/Getty Images; p.224 © Chris Jackson/Getty Images; p.228 © Ben Stansall – WPA Pool/Getty Images; p.232 © Jonathan Brady – WPA Pool/Getty Images

I owe a debt of gratitude to Marie O'Regan, the Queen's milliner, as well as to her son Stephen O'Regan. I also wish to thank Sophie Mirman, the daughter of another talented milliner, Simone Mirman, and all the designers responsible for creating the Queen's hats since the 1940s: Aage Thaarup, Claude Saint-Cyr, Frederick Fox, Philip Somerville, Valerie Lee, Angela Kelly, Stella McLaren and Rachel Trevor-Morgan.

My sincerest thanks go to Stephanie Wesle for taking the time to guide me through this fascinating world, as well as to Stefanie Stanway of the British Millinery Association. I would also like to thank Alastair Bruce for his kindly supervision, as well as the staff at *Point de Vue* magazine, of which I am proud to be a part, especially Adélaïde de Clermont-Tonnerre, Nathalie Lourau, Isabelle Rivère, François Billaut, Servane Labbé, Caroline Lazard and Hermance Murgue. I would also like to thank the cinematographer Mike Southon and Nathalie Gourseau at Palais Galliera.

Special thanks go to my editor, Boris Guilbert, without whom this book would never have seen the light of day. And to Guillaume: thank you for all your unwavering patience and support.

Thank you, lastly, to all those who contributed to this book who have chosen to remain anonymous.

Thomas Pernette

The editor wishes to extend special thanks to Isabelle Ducat.

This edition published in 2023 by Hardie Grant Books, an imprint of Hardie Grant Publishing.
First published in 2021 by Editions EPA – Hachette-Livre.
Original title: Elizabeth II Les Chapeaux de la Couronne (ISBN 978-2-37671-3-241).
All rights reserved.

Hardie Grant Books (London)
5th & 6th Floors
52–54 Southwark Street
London SE1 1UN

Hardie Grant Books (Melbourne)
Building 1, 658 Church Street
Richmond, Victoria 3121
hardiegrantbooks.com

All rights reserved. No part of this publication may be reproduced, stored in a
retrieval system ortransmitted in any form by any means, electronic, mechanical,
photocopying, recording or otherwise, without the prior written permission of the
publishers and copyright holders. The moral rights of the author have been asserted.

British Library Cataloguing-in-Publication Data. A catalogue
record for this book is available from the British Library.

Elizabeth II Les Chapeaux de la couronne© Hachette-Livre (Editions EPA), 2021

The Hats of the Queen
ISBN: 9781784886707

10 9 8 7 6 5 4 3 2 1

FOR HACHETTE LIVRE
General manager: Antoine Béon
Editorial manager: Boris Guilbert
Artistic director: Charles Ameline

Photo-engraving: Reproscan, Italie

FOR HARDIE GRANT
Publishing Director: Kajal Mistry
Acting Publishing Director: Emma Hopkin
Commissioning Editor: Kate Burkett
Proofreader: Rosie Fairhead
Translator: Victoria Weavil
Typesetter: David Meikle
Production Controller: Gary Hayes

Colour reproduction by p2d
Printed and bound in China by Leo Paper Products Ltd.